Newsmen in Khaki

★ ★ ★

Newsmen in Khaki

Tales of a World War II Soldier Correspondent

Herbert Mitgang

TAYLOR TRADE PUBLISHING
Lanham • New York • Dallas • Boulder • Toronto • Oxford

This Taylor Trade Publishing hardcover edition of *Newsmen in Khaki* is an original publication. It is published by arrangement with the author.

Published by Taylor Trade Publishing
An imprint of The Rowman & Littlefield Publishing Group, Inc.
4501 Forbes Boulevard, Suite 200
Lanham, Maryland 20706

Distributed by National Book Network

Library of Congress Cataloging-in-Publication Data

Mitgang, Herbert.
    Newsmen in khaki : tales of a World War II soldier correspondent /
Herbert Mitgang.— 1st Taylor Trade Publishing ed.
        p. cm.
    Includes index.
    ISBN 1-58979-094-4 (alk. paper)
    1. Mitgang, Herbert. 2. United States. Army Air Forces. Bomb Wing, 5th—
Biography. 3. Stars and stripes (Algiers, Algeria : Daily) 4. World War,
1939–1945—Journalism, Military—United States. 5. World War,
1939–1945—Personal narratives, American. 6. World War, 1939–1945—
Campaigns—Africa, North. 7. World War, 1939–1945—Campaigns—
Mediterranean Region. 8. Intelligence officers—United States—Biography.
9. War correspondents—United States—Biography. 10. World War, 1939–1945—
Journalists—Biography. I. Title.
D799.U6M58 2004
070.4'4994054'0092—dc22   2003026806

ALSO BY HERBERT MITGANG

HISTORY

Civilians Under Arms: Stars and Stripes, Civil War to Korea
Once Upon a Time in New York: Jimmy Walker, Franklin
    Roosevelt, and the Last Great Battle of the Jazz Age
America at Random
Spectator of America
Washington, D.C., in Lincoln's Time

BIOGRAPHY

Abraham Lincoln: A Press Portrait
The Fiery Trial: A Life of Lincoln
The Man Who Rode the Tiger: The Life and Times of
    Judge Samuel Seabury

LITERATURE

Words Still Count with Me: A Chronicle of Literary
    Conversations
Working for the Reader: A Chronicle of Culture, Literature,
    War and Politics in Books
The Letters of Carl Sandburg

REPORTAGE

Dangerous Dossiers: Exposing the Secret War against America's
    Greatest Authors
Freedom to See: Television and the First Amendment

NOVELS

The Return
Get These Men Out of the Hot Sun
The Montauk Fault
Kings in the Counting House

PLAYS

Mister Lincoln
Adlai, Alone

Dedicated to my wife, Shirley Mitgang,
who waited for me while I was overseas
for two and a half years,
and to my companions
on the Mediterranean editions of *The Stars and Stripes*,
who made life meaningful
in the midst of war
and created a higher form of military journalism
that educated and respected its uniformed readers

Contents

Gen. Eisenhower's Orders for Pvt. Mitgang

O N A SOFT spring day in 1943, toward the end of the Tunisian campaign in North Africa, I went AWOL (Absent Without Official Leave), and hitched my first airplane ride. The Germans were in retreat to the Mediterranean islands and the Italian mainland, where we and our valiant British and Canadian allies would have to fight them all over again.

The reason why I left my Army Air Corps outfit, the 5th Bombardment Wing, in Biskra, an oasis town on the northern edge of the Sahara desert, and flew to Algiers, was that I wanted to apply for a job as a soldier–correspondent with *The Stars and Stripes*, the armed forces newspaper.

If discovered, I risked being court-martialed.

About a month later these orders came through from the Adjutant General's office in Algiers to the headquarters company of the 5th Wing:

HEADQUARTERS
NORTH AFRICAN THEATER OF OPERATIONS

Private Herbert Mitgang, Army Serial Number 12085690, Headquarters Company, Fifth Wing, Army Air Corps, is hereby transferred to *The Stars and Stripes*, 10 Boulevard Baudin, Algiers.

TDN [travel directed as necessary], by air, sea, or ground transportation.

By Command of The Allied Commander-in-Chief, North Africa
Dwight D. Eisenhower
Lt. Gen., U.S. Army

(*The Stars and Stripes* was one of the independent units that, fortunately, came under the direct command of the North African Allied Commander-in-Chief's headquarters. Eisenhower proved to be a great friend of the idea of a free press for the Army newspaper, saving it from non-military censorship, demands by self-promoting officers, and preachments by chaplains.)

In a message printed in the very first issue of the Algiers edition, the trailblazing paper in North Africa, Ike wrote:

I welcome the publication of *Stars and Stripes*. We are a long way from home. Only people who have experienced the isolation inherent in extended military operations can fully appreciate the value to the soldier of news from home and friends and the need for widespread coverage of our own activities. The newspaper staff will render inestimable value to our armed forces in North Africa and to the cause for which we fight.

Eisenhower's only request was that he get a copy of the paper first thing in the morning so he could read it with his breakfast coffee. Sgt. Bill Estoff, our canny circulation manager, happily fulfilled his request and Ike became the paper's strongest fan and staunchest defender.

Through our great good fortune, in our youths our hearts were touched with fire.

— Oliver Wendell Holmes Jr.,
a wounded U. S. Civil War veteran,
Memorial Day, 1884.

★ CHAPTER 1 ★

Casablanca

Invading North Africa

M Y ORIGINAL Army outfit, the 5th Bombardment Wing, Air Corps, took part in the invasion of North Africa. I served as a sergeant in the intelligence section of the wing's headquarters company.

I had enlisted in the Army the day after I was sworn in to practice law at the Appellate Division of the New York State Supreme Court in Brooklyn. Because I strongly believed in the fight against fascism and Nazism (with its homicidal anti-Semitism and Holocaust concentration camps), I didn't wait to be drafted.

I was 22 years old, single, and hoped to do something worthwhile in uniform.

After taking written examinations at Camp Upton on Long Island, I was assigned to the Air Corps. At that time, the Air Corps was a branch of the Army and had not yet become the independent Air Force. From Camp Upton, I and other new "flyboys"—as the

1

Regular Army sergeants called us with contempt—boarded a troop train and headed for Miami and a requisitioned hotel on Biscayne Bay in Florida. There, we recruits were told to keep saluting all ranks—"You salute the uniform, not the man." Once again I was tested for my mental and mechanical capacities. After a week of drilling in the sweltering Florida summer heat, I was glad to be told that my scores qualified me to study at the Air Corps administration school, in Fort Logan, near Denver, Colorado.

In the administration school's classrooms, I learned about all the preparation and forms it took to run a fighter and bomber squadron. We were taught how to touch-type and how to keep our typewriters operating.

As our instructors repeatedly said, "It takes ten men on the ground to keep one in the air."

In one of the classes we learned how to distinguish the silhouettes of Allied and enemy aircraft flying at top speed. It was a challenge to recognize the difference between the models of a Royal Air Force Spitfire and Luftwaffe Messerschmitt.

We were trained with old British Enfield rifles. Then we were issued American Springfield rifles; the new American M-1 (Garand) rifles were reserved for infantrymen, not airmen. If the barrels of our rifles were not spotlessly clean during the daily inspections, we were penalized by not being allowed to leave Fort Logan.

Between classes, I waited on line reading *The Denver Post* and *Rocky Mountain News* to find out what was happening in the war and in the world. The New York newspapers were not available on the post. Like my fellow classmates, I wondered if I'd be going to Europe or the Pacific. On Sunday, we were given a day off. In Denver, I discovered the meaning of Western hospitality. As I strolled along the street on my first Sunday, a Cadillac pulled up alongside me. The middle-aged driver and his wife called out and invited me to have a swim and a barbecue. They asked me for my name and where I came from. These strangers seemed pleased to learn that I was a New Yorker. I hopped into the back seat. They were driving to their ranch; it included a small lake. There I was introduced to their children, was handed a bathing suit, and served a non-alcoholic drink and a non-military feast that included roasted lamb. They must have enjoyed my Brooklyn accent, and to learn that I was a newly minted lawyer, for they invited me to come again on succeeding Sundays and to bring along a Fort Logan classmate. I had made a friend—Joe Newding, from El Paso, Texas.

Our Denver hosts were happy to give a touch of home to a couple of young men; they admired the fact that we cheerfully served our country. Although I didn't consider myself patriotic, it was pleasant to hear their words and to enjoy their hospitality.

After completing my training at Fort Logan, I was ordered to go to a newly formed Air Corps bomber wing at Westover Field, Massachusetts.

Within the 5th Wing, I was assigned to the A-2 (intelligence) section of the headquarters company. The captain in charge of A-2 told me that my first assignment would be to do counterintelligence work involving our own people. I was given a secret mail address, told to do certain shadowy activities, and to tell no one what I was up to. He suggested that I should get one of the airplane mechanics to assist me, but not to give the captain the mechanic's name. No one up or down was supposed to know each other. My job was to send unfavorable information about anyone at the headquarters or on the flight line—officers or enlisted men—who expressed disloyalty to the United States. I was told that my reports would go to the Pentagon for further action. To my surprise, there were a few enemy sympathizers in our own ranks; some of them were of German or Italian heritage who had relatives in the old country.

I did send a few names to my secret mail address—it was called "The Chicopee Falls Uniform Company." Because of the sensitive nature of such accusations, these men were not allowed to remain in the Air Corps since they were considered possible security risks. Everybody knew that we would soon be going somewhere overseas to carry forward the Allied war effort.

As part of my intelligence work in the States, I also planted disinformation (although I didn't know the word's meaning then) that we were going to invade Norway. The A-2 captain I reported to had been a T-Man (Treasury agent) in Washington; he enjoyed telling me about the tricks of the trade and the need for vigilance. Of course, nobody was supposed to hear of "The Chicopee Falls Uniform Company."

Everybody in the 5th Wing was curious to know our next destination. When we were issued hats with earflaps and long johns, these items seemed to confirm that we were going to a cold climate; maybe Norway. As it turned out, North Africa that winter seemed to be near freezing, and the woolen clothing was useful; the quartermaster obviously knew something we didn't know.

Early in November 1942, the 5th Wing headquarters company boarded a troopship in New York Harbor to take part in the invasion of North Africa.

I distinctly recall taking a last look at the Statue of Liberty and wondering if I would ever see it again. Officially, nobody told us that Casablanca was our destination until we were well on our way there. The ship was the old *Santa Paula*, a converted Grace liner that had been used on the South American run. Walking around the rolling ship, I noticed that a couple of artillery pieces were manned by U. S. Navy gunners on the forward deck.

Once on the high seas well past the Narrows, the *Santa Paula* began to zigzag. Our convoy was joined by a couple of escorting Navy destroyers. As a landlubber who had never been on any ship other than the nickel-a-ride Staten Island ferry, I immediately felt my stomach churning. Instead of waiting in long lines for Army chow, I survived on chocolate bars, apples, and oranges from the PX on board the ship.

We picked up a rumor from the Navy crew: German submarines were waiting for us outside the Casablanca harbor. The convoy took evasive action and sailed down the western coast of Africa. We arrived in Casablanca in mid-November, a few days after the U-boats were gone and the shooting supposedly had stopped—but we didn't know that.

Instead of clambering up a sandy beachhead, our guys walked across the deck of a half-sunken French cruiser, the *Jean Bart*, which lay disabled in the harbor. Climbing down ladders and a gangplank, I juggled my loaded Springfield rifle (with the safety on) over my head and wore a bandoleer of ammunition across my chest.

The political situation was very tricky during and after the invasion. We didn't know if the French colonial troops, including Arabs, would greet us as liberators or were loyal to the Vichy government in German-occupied France—if it was the latter, we might be attacked. Gen. Charles de Gaulle's Free French were not yet a part of the Allied forces; his own status was uncertain.

In retrospect, I have often thought that more important than my Springfield rifle was the plastic armband I wore that was imprinted with an American flag. Surely, the fact that I was an American wearing the Stars and Stripes on my uniform was recognized as a sign of freedom and goodwill all over the world.

So I believed at that perilous moment in North Africa; and, perhaps naively, still do.

Once we found a place to bed down in Casablanca—it was on the empty shelves of a hardware store that somehow had been requisitioned by empty promises and fast-talking—we wrote letters to our folks. We had neither written home nor received any mail during the invasion blackout. All of our letters to the States were censored by junior officers in our headquarters company. I wanted to let my family and friends know where I was and that I was safe and happy. But we were not allowed to mention that the 5th Wing was momentarily located in Casablanca.

To outsmart the censors, I (and other wise guys in my outfit) wrote: "Go see a movie with Ingrid Bergman and Humphrey Bogart . . . It's got very colorful scenery."

Every such direct or indirect reference to *Casablanca* was quickly cut out.

On my second day in Casablanca, I went looking for a bookstore.

I had carried only one book with me when I enlisted: Palgrave's *Golden Treasury of the Best Songs and Lyrical Poems in the English Language*. The poems were wonderful to read while waiting on lines and by flashlight before going to sleep.

I bought up all the maps in the one Casablanca bookstore I found that showed Algeria, Morocco, and Tunisia, as well as a French-English dictionary, thinking they would be useful for our intelligence work.

I turned in the maps to the captain in charge of our intelligence section. He praised me for doing so and put a letter of commendation in my file.

A few days later I was promoted from corporal to sergeant.

★ ★ ★

Why were we in North Africa in the first place? At the time, neither the 5th Wing's officers nor those of us in the intelligence section knew.

After the war, I learned from official histories, memoirs, and the communications among the leaders of the United States, Great Britain, and the Soviet Union—Roosevelt, Churchill, and Stalin—that North Africa was the "second front" that the Allies needed to defeat Nazi Germany. The British were fighting the Afrika Corps in the desert lands between Egypt and Tunisia; on the Eastern front of the war, the Russians were resisting the Wehrmacht. To help both the British and the Russians, it was necessary to divide and draw off German forces and engage them successfully on a new battleground.

Strategically, a major D-Day invasion of German-occupied northern France, across the English Channel, was not possible as early as 1942 because of a lack of armed forces and equipment, according to Gen. Eisenhower in *Crusade in Europe*, his war memoir. Ike wrote: "The African venture was looked upon as diversionary in character in the hope that from it we would achieve great results. The least of these results was that northwest Africa would be denied to the Axis for a submarine and aircraft base. Also, that the Mediterranean could be used by the convoys of the Allied nations."

At the same time, preparations continued for the big D-Day landing in France. The combat experience gained by the Yanks and their generals fighting in Algeria and Tunisia was invaluable when the Mediterranean war moved on to Sicily and Italy. Furthermore, these battlegrounds helped to pave the way for D-Day—the main "second front" that was opened in Normandy in June 1944—and led to the final defeat of Nazi Germany.

CHAPTER 2

Oujda

"You Jew Bastard!"

CONTINUING EASTWARD toward the North African battlefront, the 5th Bomb Wing headquarters company mounted creaking "40 and 8" (forty men or eight horses) trains to Oujda, a French Foreign Legion outpost between the north-central coast and the Atlas Mountains of Morocco. The old World War I trains carried us and equipment for our bombers: B-17s (Flying Fortresses).

My pillow was a wooden box of 50-caliber ammunition—destined for our gunners—which I covered with my woolen overcoat to soften the sharp corners. A cold Sahara desert wind blew through the cracks in the cars and I wrapped my shivering body in my two mattress covers. (An old Army sergeant only half-jokingly told me: "Everyone is issued two—the first cover you fill with straw, if you can find any, to sleep on; the second cover holds your remains in case something happens to you.")

The French colonial troops stationed in Oujda shared their quarters with us, and we repaid their kindness by giving them PX chewing tobacco—which they used as pipe tobacco or rolled

into cigarettes—and tins of our rations, including surplus ched-
dar cheese.

My college French came in handy; the Frenchmen enjoyed
my English words—they were learning, too. I became friends
with a lieutenant from the 6th Regiment of Spahis (mounted
troops) and we exchanged military insignia. The officers clearly
liked Americans—their vision of us came from glamorous
Hollywood movies—and despised the Germans who had disrupted their military careers and occupied France, where their
families lived.

By now it had become clear that the Anglo-American forces
were the only hope for the survival of France and its possessions
in North Africa.

On our chow line one afternoon, I politely asked the cook who
was filling our mess kits not to give me any gravy. Not only did
he ignore my request, but he poured the dark-brown glop all
over the fried Spam that was already floating in peach juice. At
the same time, he deliberately tipped over my mess kit. It clat-
tered to the ground. The gravy spilled all over my trousers.

"You Jew bastard!" he shouted. "Don't complain about my
chow. Look at the fuckin' mess you made!"

Calling me a "Jew bastard"—those were fighting words.

I raised my fists and challenged him to come out to fight.

He reached under the mess table, picked up a stout two-by-
four, and swung it at my head. I ducked in time. Before either of
us could land a real blow, we were separated by other sergeants
on the chow line.

The cook, a semi-literate kid from Mississippi, was a Regular
Army soldier assigned to our Air Corps outfit. How did he know
I was a Jew? I didn't wear my religion on my sleeve; he had never
seen my telltale dogtags, which had the letter H (for Hebrew)

imprinted on them. He must have assumed that I was a Jew because I and several of my friends came from wicked New York and didn't speak with a Southern accent, like some of his buddies and the First Sergeant, who was from Georgia.

In the 1940s, religious and racial prejudice existed in many professions and bastions of American life, including colleges and resorts. I first observed it at the requisitioned Army Air Corps hotel in Biscayne Bay, Florida, where I was first stationed.

Leafing through the hotel's prewar brochure, I came across the word "Restricted"—which, of course, meant that no Jews and surely no Negroes or Latinos would be allowed to stay there as paying guests.

A beautiful irony! Thanks to the Air Corps, I was sleeping in a bedroom that the hotel's owners would not allow me to stay in for pay in civilian life. For the hell of it, I told the hotel's manager and flunkies that I was one of their "Restricted" guests. They acted as if they didn't know what I was talking about.

The day after the near-fight with the ignorant cook from Mississippi, I was reported to the 5th Wing's personnel officer by the First Sergeant, a Regular Army man, who was waiting to throw the book at one of the new sergeants. As he often told us, it had taken him three hitches—nine years—to make sergeant. I had been promoted to sergeant in six months.

The First Sergeant claimed that he had witnessed my encounter with the cook, but not that he had heard me called a "Jew bastard." Of course, he was lying.

Like the dumb cook, the First Sergeant spoke in Army lingo. He woke us up by screaming: "Grab your socks and drop your cocks!"

The topkick couldn't remember anyone's name. He called you "Private Shithead" or "Corporal Shithead" or "Sergeant Shithead." All enlisted men were "shitheads" and all lieutenants were "fuckfaces." That about completed his vocabulary.

I thought: If four-letter words were taken out of the topkick's mouth, he'd be speechless.

Two days after my encounter with the cook, the First Sergeant told me that, under Army regulations in his man's Army, a non-commissioned officer was not allowed to challenge or fight with a private. He demanded that I be disciplined—to show his authority and as an example to all the other corporals and sergeants—by taking away my stripes.

He ordered the company clerk to post my name on a makeshift bulletin board as a disciplinary case by his personal orders. No commissioned officers were around to challenge him.

Without any chance to present my case or appeal the decision to higher-ups, I found myself busted from sergeant back to private.

I never wrote home to tell my family or friends what had happened. I felt heartbroken.

CHAPTER 3

Biskra, Algeria

The Bombfighter Bulletin

W HEN I HITCHED my first airplane ride from Biskra, the oasis town on the northern edge of the Sahara Desert in Algeria, where the 5th Bomb Wing was stationed, to Algiers, I had never known that *The Stars and Stripes* existed in the North African theater of operations.

I vaguely recalled reading that during World War I, an American Army newspaper with that name had been published in Paris, and its managing editor was Sgt. Harold Ross, who later founded *The New Yorker*.

An early edition of the weekly *Stars and Stripes*, edited and printed in Algiers, reached Biskra in the spring of 1943. It was shown to me by a sympathetic friend, Lt. Ben Z. Kaplan, a respected administrative officer at wing headquarters.

"Why don't you go to Algiers and apply for a job on the paper?" he suggested. "I wish I could, but I think that everyone on the staff has to be an enlisted man." He was more than half-right;

two of the older sergeants with newspaper experience had been advanced to lieutenant.

I loved his idea but wondered if I could get permission from my First Sergeant, the chickenshit Regular Army ignoramus, to leave our headquarters for a day or two.

"Go ahead," Lt. Kaplan said. "I'll cover up for you in case anyone discovers that you're missing. I'll say that you're on assignment from me to arrange for distribution of the paper to the 5th Wing, which is a good thing to do anyway."

I thanked him and took my first ride the next day in a C-47, a two-engine transport plane. Sitting in a bucket seat, I looked out the window and saw the propellers twirling and watched the figures on the ground grow smaller and smaller. So this is what it was like in the Air Corps. I hoped the Luftwaffe wasn't anywhere near our unarmed plane.

In Algiers, I thumbed my way from the airfield at Maison Blanche to the offices of *The Stars and Stripes* at No. 10 Boulevard Baudin.

Without any appointment, I was interviewed by the chief editor, First Lieutenant (eventually Lt. Col.) Robert Neville, a brilliant journalist whose experiences included working as foreign editor of *Time*, for the *New York Herald Tribune* and for *PM*, the ad-less newspaper in New York.

He introduced himself as Bob Neville—I discovered that everyone was on a first-name basis at the paper and that nobody pulled rank. Naturally, I built up my credentials. Before going to law school, I had been a college newspaper editor and also an occasional sports stringer for the *Brooklyn Eagle*. Even in law school, I had dreamed of becoming a newspaperman.

"What I need around here are editors to help me put out the paper," Lt. Neville said. "Some of the boys on the staff don't even know how to spell Hitler's first name."

I shivered in my boots, hoping he wouldn't ask me. Was the newspaper's own style anglicized to Adolph or still Adolf?

He added, "All the editors want to go up front and be byliners like Ernie Pyle and the other big-name civilian correspondents. You wouldn't mind staying right here in the home office as an editor and writer, would you?"

"Sure," I quickly replied. "That's just what I've been doing at the 5th Wing—putting out a little mimeographed newspaper called *The Bombfighter Bulletin*."

I showed him a copy and told him that I was its sole reporter and editor.

That did it. We shook hands and he said my transfer would be coming through in about a month. He liked the idea of having an Air Corps man on the staff.

At that moment, I felt like the luckiest soldier in North Africa.

I continued my duties in the wing's intelligence section. Our Flying Fortresses were hitting the fleeing German transports in Tunis and Bizerte. The last bomber on a mission took photographs of the damage. It was our task to determine the effectiveness of the bombing. Fortunately, one of my colleagues was a mapmaker who had worked for the U.S. Geodetic Survey. He did most of the work and taught me how to study the photographic images through a stereoscope.

I also did liaison work with the loyal Free French colonial forces; they were on the lookout for any Germans who might have slipped through the front lines to try to sabotage our aircraft. The native troops knew every *djebel* and *wadi* around our airfield.

And I took my turn pulling guard duty. One time, after midnight, I saw what I thought was an unfriendly Arab in a white burnoose crawling toward me. I clicked off the safety on my rifle, then regretted doing so because it made such a loud noise in the still of the night that it gave away my position. Suddenly, the crawling image barked; it turned out to be a stray dog. Back went the safety. Lucky dog!

The most exciting moment at our headquarters in Biskra came when Margaret Bourke-White, the famous *Life* magazine photographer, visited the 5th Wing. We could not help staring at the rare sight of a beautiful American woman in the oasis town where neither a nurse nor a Red Cross girl was stationed. To be in her presence, all the officers and enlisted men volunteered to carry her camera equipment.

She had talked herself into photographing a bombing mission. Col. Joseph Atkinson, the 5th Wing's commanding officer, who was movie-handsome, outranked everyone else; she flew in his lead plane during the bombing of targets in Tunisia.

I heard a couple of pilots wondering where Miss Bourke-White would sleep and go to the bathroom while with the 5th Wing. In view of our primitive facilities, that seemed to be a more fundamental concern than whether her life might be in danger during the flight over enemy-held territory. She bravely flew on the daylight bombing mission and returned with a series of aerial photographs that appeared in *Life* a few weeks later.

As for her personal comfort, it became common knowledge around the headquarters that she stayed with Col. Atkinson in his hotel room in Biskra. We later learned that it was the beginning of a beautiful wartime romance.

A month before my fateful trip to Algiers, I had started *The Bombfighter Bulletin*, with the encouragement and support of Lt. Kaplan. The reason for its name was that the 5th Bomb Wing had added two fighter groups to escort our two groups of Flying Fortresses.

My aim as editor was to report the combat achievements of our airmen who were risking their lives almost every flying day, rather than reporting only the activities of the headquarters company or the 12th Air Force, which was commanded by the heroic Gen. Jimmy Doolittle, who had led the daring raid on Tokyo in retaliation for the attack on Pearl Harbor. President Roosevelt said that the Doolittle raid was the first good news he had received in the White House since the beginning of the war.

I also wanted to give my readers news about what was going on in the States and on the other battlefronts around the world.

I needed transportation to get out to the wing's airstrips before the bombing targets were chosen and during the debriefings after the missions. I knew the best stories would come from the pilots, navigators, and gunners.

Standing alongside the ground crews, I joined them in song:

Off they go
into the wild blue yonder,
off with one helluva roar.
Off they go
into the wild blue yonder,
climbing high into the sun.
At 'em, boys, give 'er the gun.
We live in fame
or go down in flame
But nothing'll stop the Army Air Corps!

After the mission, I stood counting our bombers as they flew home, hoping that the same number returned as had taken off. Some were badly peppered with enemy flak, but the B-17 was a sturdy plane that could stay aloft, as the pilots said, "on a wing and a prayer."

No jeep was available for me, so I requisitioned a bicycle from a store in Biskra, signing a piece of paper which promised the owner that he would be compensated after the war by the U.S. government. (I hope he's not still waiting to be paid.) It was a broken down two-wheeler, with its tires punctured; there were no replacements. I rode the bike on its rims.

To gather national and foreign news for my small paper, I dropped in at the Wing's radio shack at night and tuned in to the BBC broadcasts from London. (Ever since then, I've hoped that the high standards of the BBC could be replicated for national public radio and television stations in the United States.) I also listened to the propaganda spewed by "Axis Sally" over Radio Berlin and cautioned my readers who heard her on short-wave radios not to listen to her lies about German victories. Occasionally, old copies of *Time* turned up at our headquarters and I rewrote some of the magazine's pieces for *The Bombfighter Bulletin*.

Then I typed the two-page newsletter in hand-drawn columns on a stencil and cranked out a few hundred copies by hand.

Finally, I rode out to the 5th's bomber and fighter groups on my bike and distributed the paper—it was, of course, free.

On the paper's masthead, Lt. Ben Z. Kaplan was listed as publisher and Pvt. Herbert Mitgang as editor.

A typical issue of the spring 1943 *Bombfighter Bulletin* included stateside news headlined:

★ ★ ★

THE HOME FRONT

Washington, D.C.—Congress has agreed on compromise tax legislation—but only temporarily. The plan would cancel a full year's taxes for persons owing $50 or less. The 25 percent that must be paid is payable over 1944–1945. Beginning July 1, 20 percent will be deducted from every person's salary, after a few basic exemptions are allowed.

Explaining the effect that the compromise tax plan would have on men in the armed forces, President Roosevelt said:

"A substantial part of the cost of the war will be transferred from the upper income to the middle and lower income groups. Our soldiers on the battlefronts are among those who would later be obliged to shoulder the cost from which our more fortunate taxpayers have been relieved."

Legislators on the Senate finance committee said that the debate will continue in order to relieve soldiers, sailors, and airmen from tax obligations incurred while serving overseas.

★ ★ ★

In another Washington development in the foreign policy field, President Roosevelt approved an American–Chinese treaty in which the United States relinquished all of its extra-territorial rights in China.

★ ★ ★

Tin Pan Alley: Sgt. Paul Reiff, the tunesmith famous for his "Isle of Capri," has just composed music to "Dirty Gertie from Bizerte." The bawdy GI poem by Pvt. William Russell is expected to become a hit with music distributors in Tin Pan Alley, New York.

(The opening lines go: "Dirty Gertie from Bizerte / Hid a mousetrap 'neath her skirtie . . .")

Predicts Sgt. Reif, who is stationed in Algiers, "A victory by the United Nations will result in new forms of happy, jazzy, frivolous popular music after the war."

Rank and file: The first recorded case because of jealousy due to Army rank landed one sergeant and a lieutenant in a Miami divorce court. The lieutenant was Army nurse Betty Rachford La Macchia and the sergeant was her husband, Joe La Macchia. Betty charged her husband with extreme cruelty because he was jealous of her higher rank. She said he resented the fact that she fraternized with officers at clubs where he was barred.

The main news in *The Bombfighter Bulletin* concerned the activities of our Air Corps units. Sometimes the items I wrote appeared under the heading "Vapor Trails"—a title I would occasionally use later in *The Stars and Stripes* magazine section in Italy.

VAPOR TRAILS

A Salute to the Air Corps Mechanics

A pilot walked over to a knot of mechanics at an airfield on the Tunisian front.

"Say, what did you guys use to patch the flak holes on my plane?"

"I patched some with the bottoms of five-gallon tins," said T-Sgt. John T. King of Fort Worth.

"I used linen patching like they used on fabric ships before airplanes were made of metal," explained T-Sgt. Harry C. Engle of Chicago.

"Holy smoke!" said the pilot, squinting down at a patch. (He preferred not to reveal his name for fear that his family might worry that he got shot up on missions.) "Will they hold?"

The mechanics reassured him that their makeshift patches would hold for months.

A few minutes later, another formation of bombers was being beaded together after returning from a Mediterranean hot spot between Tunis and Sicily to knock out the precious shipping needed by the Axis forces to supply their Tunisian campaign against the Anglo-American troopers.

"A kit with between 100 and 200 special tools is considered the minimum with which to maintain our planes," said Warrant Officer George O'Dell of Republic, Mo. "Yet I remember when two of our air crew chiefs set out to repair a plane with only a pair of diagonals, a crescent wrench, a screw driver, and a pair of pliers to do it with."

Spare parts were nonexistent in the first months of the Tunisian campaign. So when a plane returned too shot up or had to make a belly landing, mechanics swarmed all over it. These disabled planes served as "warehouses" of spare parts for bombers still able to fly.

Changing tires on the big planes looks impossible without the big wing and nose jacks that are standard equipment in the Air Corps in the States. To change a nose wheel tire the mechanics raised the nose by having ten men get into the tail of the plane.

One time during a period of bad weather, the group was asked to bomb an Axis airfield near Tunis. Pilots were willing to fly, but the vital rubber de-icer boots on some of the planes were in bad shape and needed patching. Rubber was scarce. Finally a young mechanic hit on a solution. Several rubber life vests, the famous "Mae Wests," were torn up and the rubber used to patch the de-icer boots.

The mission went out on schedule and caught thirteen Axis fighter planes on the ground.

When my transfer orders to *The Stars and Stripes*, countersigned by Lt. Gen. Eisenhower, the Allied commander-in-chief in the North African Theater of Operations, arrived at the 5th's headquarters, I was summoned to the office of our commanding officer, Col. Atkinson, a dashing flier whose wings showed that he was a command pilot.

"What's this all about, Mitgang?"

I mumbled that I was pleased to go to the big-time newspaper in Algiers for all the armed forces—including the Air Corps—in North Africa.

Col. Atkinson said that not only did he like *The Bombfighter Bulletin*, but so did his boss, Gen. Jimmy Doolittle, the 12th Air Force commander.

He urged me to stay with the 5th Wing and continue to put out my little mimeographed newspaper.

If I remained, he promised that I would get sergeant's stripes immediately. When I hesitated, Col. Atkinson added that he would then give me a "battlefield commission" as a second lieutenant.

"Think about it overnight, Mitgang, and let me know your decision first thing in the morning so I can get these orders countermanded and put through your promotion," Col. Atkinson said, and extended his hand.

I left his office both pleased and confused.

When I spoke to Lt. Kaplan about Col. Atkinson's offer, he said he knew all about it. I asked him—as a friend—for his advice.

"Go to *Stars and Stripes*," Ben said, "and I wish I could go with you."

That settled it in my mind.

The next day, Col. Atkinson was leading a bombing mission so I left word with his aide of my decision and told him to thank the colonel for me.

My departure marked the end of *The Bombfighter Bulletin*.

Several days later, I said my goodbyes to friends at Wing headquarters.

The last one I saw was Hammed, an Arab shoeshine boy who had attached himself to me after I gave him a weekly ration of chocolate bars. Hammed insisted that I accompany him to a street market in the Arab quarter before we parted. There he bought me a local delicacy—a paper cone filled with fried grasshoppers. To show me how good they tasted, he ate a few himself. I could hear the grasshopper wings crunching between his teeth.

I didn't want to reject his kindness, so I pointed to my stomach and said I was full and would save the fried grasshoppers to eat later.

When Hammed was out of sight, I dug a hole with my sheath knife and buried his gift.

The next day I went out to the airfield and thumbed a ride (it was that easy as long as you had orders) on a two-engine C-47, which the Brits called a Dakota, that was going to Algiers. Although I didn't know it at the time, I would soon begin a new military life—and a new career in civilian life afterward.

CHAPTER 4

Algiers

On *The Stars and Stripes*

FTER SLEEPING under canvas and eating out of a mess kit with the 5th Wing's headquarters company, living in the requisitioned *Stars and Stripes* building in Algiers that we shared with charming, dedicated American Red Cross girls was like being upgraded to a five-star luxury caravansary in New York or London.

We had a special friend and ally—Janice Duncan, a vivacious Red Cross volunteer, who was married to Sgt. Gregor Duncan, one of our talented staff artists. (Greg was later killed on the Anzio beachhead in Italy.)

Our editorial and mechanical staffs slept in beds with mattresses and ate in a dining hall on white tablecloths with regular plates and silverware. Our Army rations were supplemented by local produce. We were served by local waitresses.

"How would you like your eggs this morning, monsieur?"

"Scrambled, but not powdered, mademoiselle. Merci."

★ ★ ★

I later learned that *The Stars and Stripes* had a venerable history.

Our edition in North Africa followed in the footsteps of a noble military newspaper tradition. All of us on the Algiers edition thought that our sole predecessor was the newspaper with the same name published in Paris during the First World War.

Actually, in researching the historical origins of *Stars and Stripes* after the war, I discovered that during the Civil War, Union Army printers put out several editions, coincidentally called *The Stars and Stripes,* in captured enemy newspaper plants. None were related except by name.

(I could find no such publication during the Revolutionary War. Thomas Paine's influential pamphlet, *Common Sense,* served as vital reading material in the ranks.)

The Stars and Stripes was published for the first time by four Union enlisted men in 1861, in Bloomfield, Missouri. Other Civil War editions, carrying "Stars and Stripes" on their mastheads, were published in Jacksonport, Arkansas; New Orleans; and Thibodaux, Louisiana. In at least one case—because no newsprint was available—the paper was printed on the reverse side of floral wallpaper that had been ripped off the walls in Confederate territory. (This information about the Civil War editions was originally unearthed by C. E. Dornbusch of the New York Public Library. Neither Dornbusch nor I could find a rebel paper called *Stars and Bars* or any other named to resemble the controversial Confederate battle flag that is flaunted by Lost Cause segregationists in the Deep South to this day.)

Here is a description of the mind of the Union rifleman (familiarly called Billy Yank) as described in this unsigned piece in a Civil War edition of *The Stars and Stripes.* Billy Yank's deadly honesty reminds me of the embattled GI Joes I encountered in North Africa and Italy.

HOW A MAN FEELS IN BATTLE

There can be nothing more puzzling than the analysis of one's feelings on a battlefield. You cannot describe them to yourself or others. To march steadily straight up to the mouths of a hundred cannon, while they pour out fire and smoke and shot and shell in a storm that mows the men like grass, is horrible beyond description—appalling. It is absurd to say a man can do it without fear.

During [General Winfield Scott] Hancock's charge at Fredericksburg, for a long distance the slope was swept by such a hurricane of death that we thought every step would be our last, and I am willing to admit that I was pretty badly scared. Whatever may be said about getting used to it, old soldiers secretly dread a battle equally with new ones. But the most difficult thing to stand up under is the suspense while waiting, drawn up in line of battle on the edge of the field, watching the columns file past us and disappear in a cloud of smoke, where horses and men and colors go down in confusion, where all sounds are lost in the screaming of shells, the cracking of musketry, the thunder of artillery, and knowing that our turn comes next, expecting each moment the word "Forward!"

It brings a strange kind of relief when "Forward" comes. You move mechanically with the rest. Once fairly in for it, your sensibilities are strangely blunted—you care comparatively nothing about the sights that shocked you at first—men torn to pieces by cannon shot become a matter of course. At such a time there comes a latent sustenance from within us.

Those who say they would like to visit a battlefield seldom know what they are talking about. After darkness has put an end to the struggle, a hush settles over the field—such a contrast to the roar of the fight! Never is silence more oppressive, more eloquent. You hear the cries of the wounded. A stray shot hurls through the darkness overhead. You hear the ambulance chirr heavily along, grinding through the soil with a sullen muffled sound, like some monster crunching the bones of its victims. You see the outlines of forms gliding through the gloom, carrying on litters pale, bloody men. You stumble over—perhaps your friend—with his hair matted in blood over his white face, and his dead eyes staring blindly up to the sky.

Then talk about the horrors of war.

During World War I, seventy-one issues of *The Stars and Stripes* were published in Paris between February 8, 1918, and June 13, 1919, for combat and occupation troops. Sgt. Harold Ross (the future founding editor of *The New Yorker* magazine) was the editor. The staff included Pvts. Hudson Hawley and John T. Winterich and Sgt. Alexander Woolcott (the *New York Times* drama critic and essayist). Two officers also wrote for the paper: Lt. Grantland Rice (a renowned sports writer) and Capt. Franklin P. Adams (known as F.P.A., whose popular New York newspaper column, "The Conning Tower," featured essays and poems by himself and outside contributors).

The pioneering Paris *Stars and Stripes* carried advertising—mostly for cigarettes: "I'd walk a mile for a CAMEL." (No ads appeared in the World War II editions.)

The paper set the pattern of praising the enlisted men rather than serving as a bulletin board for official documents. Under Sgt. Ross's editorship, the news dispatches about the exploits of the A.E.F. (American Expeditionary Force) emphasized storytelling.

The Algiers edition that I happily joined in the spring of 1943 was an offshoot of the first *Stars and Stripes* that was published during World War II in London.

At the offices and plant of *The London Times*, 915 issues of *Stripes* (as we sometimes called it for short) were produced, beginning in the spring of 1942. The paper was especially strong on covering the activities of the U.S. 8th Air Force in England. Several of the reporters flew on the bombers that were engaged in dangerous missions attacking military targets in Germany and Nazi-occupied Europe. (After the war, Andy Rooney became the best-known member of the London edition. He created the role of essayist for *60 Minutes* on CBS television.)

After the North African invasion, a small contingent of officers and enlisted men flew from London to Algiers to investigate the possibility of starting a new edition there.

They were led by Col. Egbert White and included Staff Sgt. Robert Neville. Bert White had been an enlisted man, handling circulation for *Stars and Stripes* in Paris during World War I. In civilian life between the wars, he was a successful advertising executive. When World War II began, he convinced Pentagon officials that the Americans serving overseas should have their own newspaper and volunteered to start *Stars and Stripes*. Bob Neville was a seasoned writer and editor who had been a foreign correspondent for *Time* and had also written for *PM*, the ad-less newspaper in New York that attracted some of the best journalists in the United States.

Col. White remained in Algiers as commanding officer of the new edition. When he turned 49, we gave him a birthday party in our newsroom. Sgt. Neville, who also decided not to return to London, became editor, and within two weeks received a "battlefield commission" as a lieutenant. He was in his thirties; most of us were in our twenties.

A month after the North African invasion, on December 9, 1942, the first issue of the weekly Algiers edition began publishing— eventually 461 daily and weekly issues were printed at the plant of L'Echo d'Alger. The GI linotypists and makeup men were recruited by Sgt. Irving Levinson, an experienced printer in civilian life, who soon doubled as First Sergeant as well as mechanical foreman, with the rank of master sergeant.

The Algiers edition concentrated on covering the ground war—the campaign by the infantry and armored divisions against the Germans in Tunisia.

Among those serving as combat correspondents at the front in Tunisia were Sgts. Jack Foisie and Ralph G. Martin. Our photographer was Sgt. Phil Stern, who insisted on getting close to the action with the U. S. Rangers; he suffered shrapnel wounds, but got remarkable pictures.

As Bob Neville repeated when I joined the staff, "All the boys want to cover the front, but I need editors to help me put out the paper." I did editing and also wrote local features.

After Col. White returned to the States, Bob Neville was promoted a rank at a time and wound up a lieutenant colonel and the officer in charge, overseeing a half-dozen editions of *Stars and Stripes.*

Not until the war moved across the Mediterranean to Sicily and the Italian mainland did I get my turn to cover the front. By then, beginning in the summer of 1943 and all during 1944, I had done my editing duties as managing editor of the Oran and Palermo (Sicily) editions, and could assign myself to reporting stories all around the growing Mediterranean theater of operations.

The staff of the Algiers edition initiated other editions in North Africa—in Oran, Casablanca, and Tunis—and quickly followed the combat troops across the Mediterranean with more new editions. By then, most of us were old pros at putting out newspapers in foreign plants.

Of course, the men on *Stripes* weren't the only ones sharpening their skills. So were the riflemen and generals, including Omar

Bradley and George Patton—both later led battle-hardened armies in France under Gen. Eisenhower because they had proved themselves in North Africa.

The reporters and editors of the London edition of *Stars and Stripes* also began to develop new offshoots. Appropriately, the first "Continental edition" began publishing on July 4, 1944, printed at L'Eclair, in Cherbourg, France. A Brittany edition was started in August 1944, printed at L'Ouest, in Rennes. Following the liberation of Paris, 493 issues were printed between September 5, 1944 and February 1, 1946 at the plant of the *New York Herald Tribune*.

After a second invasion took place in southern France, staffers from the Mediterranean edition in Rome as well as staffers from London established new editions as the Allied forces moved closer to Germany. These included papers in Grenoble, Besancon, Strasbourg, Dijon, and Nancy.

In Belgium, an edition was created in Liege, where eighty-eight issues were printed at La Meuse, beginning January 20, 1945.

Once inside Germany, as the fighting subsided and the occupation began, staffers following the victorious troops started a paper in Pfungstadt—beginning April 5, 1945, with 370 issues printed at the Frankfurter Zeitung. And in southern Germany, beginning May 8, 1945, 567 issues were printed at Nurnberg Uhr Blatt, in Altdorf, Bavaria.

I once asked Col. Bob Neville why there wasn't a *Stars and Stripes* in the Pacific Theater. He surmised that first, there was no tradition to follow in the Pacific, and, second, Gen. Douglas MacArthur would not encourage a GI paper that he couldn't control. "We were lucky to have Ike as our commanding general," Bob said.

Eventually, a Middle Pacific edition of *Stars and Stripes* was initiated toward the end of the war on May 14, 1945, and it continued publishing until January 30, 1946. About 222 issues were printed on the presses of the *Honolulu Advertiser* in Hawaii.

A peacetime European edition of *The Stars and Stripes* continued to be published in Germany. The masthead carried an ambiguous phrase to describe its supervision: "An authorized unofficial publication."

This curious disclaimer was defined this way: "*The Stars and Stripes* is published in conjunction with the armed forces information program of the Department of Defense. Contents are not necessarily the official view of the U. S. Government, Department of Defense, or the U.S. European Command."

As I ponder these words, I cannot help thinking how lucky my companions and I were in wartime North Africa and Italy.

We wrote what we pleased, we became pretty good newspapermen, did something important for the Allied cause, and all our readers—both officers and enlisted men—admired our paper. And we had a lot of fun!

I was curious to find out if the Germans also put out a newspaper for their troops and, if so, what kind of news it carried. A copy of the enemy's paper—it was called *Oase*—turned up in a prisoner-of-war camp. It was little more than a propaganda sheet that carried relatively no news.

Most of the enemy weekly was filled with ranting attacks on the American government and at Jews.

In this propaganda organ, Field Marshal Erwin Rommel's vaunted Afrika Corps was imbued with the Third Reich's official anti-Semitism. Here is an extract from the German paper:

The Americans in Algiers and their Jewish emigrant apes are composing leaflet after leaflet, working their fingers to the bones, and wracking their brains over the great question of how to capture a German soldier, or best of all, a whole German panzer army at once.

Well now, my dear stupid Americans, the German mail service is in good condition and the people of the Fatherland know exactly how many tanks, cannon, coffee beans, English cigarettes, American comic magazines as well as numberless leaflets have fallen into the hands of us 'doomed ones.'

This phony German Army newspaper was not published in the field, but produced in Berlin by Josef Goebbels, Hitler's propaganda minister.

Bob Neville wanted our soldier paper in Algiers to be as professional as the civilian publications in the States. Actually, because we carried no advertising, the daily eight-page *Stars and Stripes* was full of news—more than most hometown papers carried.

In Algiers—to make sure that we enlisted men were not harassed by higher-ranking officers or got swelled heads because some of us wore insignia on our uniforms saying we were *Stars and Stripes* correspondents, one day Col. White decided to remind us that we were still in the U.S. Army. He ordered the entire staff to do calisthenics on the roof of our requisitioned building. So after hopping out of bed in our undershorts, we stretched our straining muscles while French residents in nearby apartment houses watched with smiles of amusement as the "crazy Americans" did pushups in the chilling morning cold.

The exercises were led by First Sgt. Irv Levinson. An unwilling disciplinarian with a hearty laugh and a generous nature, Irv had been a respected printer in civilian life. As mechanical foreman, his main job was to find and supervise GI makeup men, Linotype operators, photoengravers, and stereotypers who knew how to produce a newspaper on the presses of *L'Echo d'Alger*, an independent French daily located on the Rue de la Liberté, where *Stars and Stripes* was printed.

No distinction was made at our dining tables between officers and enlisted men. We constantly talked about ways to improve our coverage—how to play the stories by our own daring combat correspondents who practically lived with the infantry divisions on the Tunisian battlegrounds, add stories about the Navy and Air Corps, obtain more Washington news, and include the activities of the less-glamorous service outfits in the rear echelon that stretched from Algiers in both directions across Morocco and Algeria.

As a novice, I listened closely, hoping to pick up the rhythm of the paper and, incidentally, to learn what kind of stories I might contribute when I wasn't busy editing and assembling a page of news about the United States. On the desk, I enjoyed writing headlines that could capture the attention of our readers.

Our aim as reporters and editors was both to inform and educate the Joes and Janes (there was a company of the Women's Army Corps—the Wacs) about North Africa and the other Allied theaters of warfare. We also sought information about what veterans might expect after the war, and the prospects for the United Nations in the postwar world. Although the U.N. was not yet formally established, it already was referred to as the United Nations in the Algiers edition.

Like most of my colleagues on the editorial staff, I was aware that *Stars and Stripes* was creating a higher standard of military journalism that differed from Army base newspapers in the States, and that we were recording history where it was being made overseas.

I became interested in learning the mechanics of producing the Algiers weekly edition—the composition of the paper by our own printers who knew how to operate the hot-type Linotype machines, the makeup of the pages on the "stone" in the composing room, the stereotyping of the matrixes, and the printing on the rotary presses of *L'Echo d'Alger*.

Many of the soldier-printers recruited by Sgt. Levinson flashed their union cards from the ITU (International Typographical Union) to prove that they knew their stuff and were real journeymen. Ours was practically a union shop because a number of the printers had worked on newspapers in New York, Chicago, and other cities. The printers loved to correct the editors about what they considered the right style and typography for our five-column, tabloid-size *Stars and Stripes* editions

Standing on my side of the "stone" opposite the makeup man, I learned how to read the type upside down and backwards, cut stories and eliminate "widows" to make a perfect fit, and improve the looks of a page as it was assembled in a "chase." Then I asked the makeup man for proofs to get a last look for my final okay before the pages were locked up and rolled away.

The French foremen in the composing room listened in wonder to Irv Levinson's diplomatic demands, in his limited French, that they bring out their newest, unbroken typefaces for the American Army newspaper. Levinson's supply of PX tobacco and goodies helped them to cooperate.

Friendships were established in the composing room and soon the French foremen were repeating, in accented English, Irv's favorite expression, "Oh, my aching back!"

★ ★ ★

Gen. Eisenhower's headquarters were located in the St. George, the grandest hotel in Algiers, and his staff was a source of official news as well as aid when we needed transportation and living quarters.

Ike let us know that he thought well of the coverage by *Stars and Stripes*. When necessary, we quoted him: "This newspaper should be the equivalent of a soldier's hometown paper, with no censorship of its contents other than for security."

Our commanding officers, Col. White and Capt. Neville, invoked Ike's name when expanding the staff to start new editions of the paper in Oran, Casablanca, and Tunis after it was captured. Soon we turned the Algiers weekly into a daily newspaper.

Once the Allies securely held North Africa, our thoughts turned to the next beachheads on the mainland of Nazi-occupied Europe. In a rare editorial for the Algiers edition, Sgt. Milton Lehman decided to put these thoughts into print to show that American minds were never far from home. (Lehman became a renowned magazine writer after the war.) He called his eloquent essay for the Algiers weekly a "Letter to America."

LETTER TO AMERICA

By Sgt. Milton Lehman

We are waiting the long days to D-Day,
the last hours to H-Hour,
We are waiting in canvas tents above the beaches,
the beaches we took in November
as a beginning to these days,
the beaches we took in the march to the east,

the beaches we took in the last weeks
of the great push.
And now we are waiting and looking across the sea
and running the ramrod through our M-1s
and counting our rifle clips and
watching the flick of sun on our bayonets.
We are well, America, and we are ready.
We are waiting for the signal.
The future belongs to us now
and we are waiting to meet it.
In November we came to a continent with a Blue Book
telling us what to do, what to say, how to say it,
but when we hit the beaches we forgot the Blue Book,
and we did it our own way, said it our own way
and in our own voice,
and the people were glad to see us
and we made ourselves at home.
We came here with weapons that did not weigh us down
but made us stronger:
With the howitzer of the Maine farm on our backs,
the good soil, and the corn stalks and the cool rains,
With the mortar of the Shenandoah Valley,
and HE shells of red oak, white pine, and blue rivers,
We carried hand grenades of Scranton coal
and Alabama cotton bolls
And battering rams of Oregon sequoia.
Thinking of home while we fought
in the djebels and wadis of Tunisia, new
thoughts came to us and we remember them:
The world must build a new house, America,
a house big enough for all the peoples to live in.
(For we on the beaches of Africa are waiting now,
to splinter the old house, crash in its weak rafters,

rip up its rotten floorboards
open it up to the sky.)
There will be many residents in the new house, America:
the British, who fight with endless determination;
the Chinese, who fight with
the strength of generations,
the Russians, who fight with iron faith
in their vast land,
the French, who fight to bring their land to life;
the conquered peoples of the slave states,
saddled with Quislings, betrayers, spies,
waiting now to get a fighting chance;
and the people of the Axis, of the losing fight,
who must be brought once more
into the house.
A house so great will need firm foundations, America,
and the foundations we remember
in your hills and valleys; the concrete of the
structure needs firm lumber from
your tall, benevolent trees to make the form;
water from cool and tolerant streams to make the mix;
granite from your deepest quarries
for toughness and strength;
and hardening by your warm and
overseeing sun.
It is time to begin the foundations now,
time to draw up the blueprint
The blueprint, America, must be drawn to the
right proportions this time.

It is ironic to read the above idealistic thoughts today without
thinking of the Cold War and the reactionary forces that shat-

tered many of these dreams in the United States and elsewhere around the globe, where fundamental freedoms could not be enjoyed by all the peoples, where an Iron Curtain was erected, where anti-Semitism and racism still existed, and religious, ethnic, and tribal conflicts continued, despite the existence of the United Nations.

Algiers served as a rest center for troops on leave and *Stars and Stripes* printed a column called "Yank About Town" and a datebook that told where recreational facilities were located. Some soldiers attended church and synagogue services; it was a good way to meet families and be invited to their homes for a festive meal.

At Franco-American social events attended by some *Stars and Stripes* staffers seeking companionship, my friends and I sometimes used a favorite line with the Mademoiselles and their ever-present chaperons. It went:

"Je ne suis pas un simple soldat. Je suis un correspondent de guerre." (I'm not an ordinary soldier. I'm a war correspondent.)

At the same time, the French people were struggling with American slang. Striking up a conversation, they invariably said: "You speak me, Joe." (Apparently, they thought every soldier was familiarly called "Joe.")

We sometimes parodied them amongst ourselves: "You speak me, Herb." "Non, you speak me first, John."

The heart and soul of the American GI came through honestly, humorously, and sentimentally in the verse he (and sometimes she—nurses and members of the Women's Army Corps) wrote for a regular feature called "Puptent Poets" that appeared in almost every issue of *Stars and Stripes.*

(Gripes were reserved for the daily "Mail Call" column.) Dozens of poems were submitted to the paper every week. The poems were either accepted or politely rejected by Cpl. John Welsh III, an aesthetic Harvard graduate, who was our full-time poetry editor.

Welsh—a good friend who had been with me in the 5th Wing—said that he wasn't looking for poet laureates, but rather for authentic voices coming from the foxholes and hospital wards. Some of the poems arrived on bloodstained paper.

Here's a sampling of what appeared in "Puptent Poets."

(After the war, the first poet here, Sgt. Peter Viereck, won the Pulitzer Prize for his verse.)

MINE LAYERS

"Ripeness Is All"

Through nights of slanting rain
Marchers are planting pain
Gardeners in boots
Plant tender seeds of mines
Where the dimmed flashlight shines
Nursing the wire-vines,
Hiding the roots.
Boys in green raincoats scamper
Where grass will soon be damper
With sudden red.
Ripe, ripe the pain grows high
Sudden into the sky. . .
New-mown the new crops lie,
Earth's new-mown dead.

—Sgt. Peter Viereck

★ ★ ★

DIRTY GERTIE

Dirty Gertie from Bizerte
Hid a mousetrap 'neath her skertie,
Strapped it on her kneecap purty
Baited it wth Fleur de Flirte,
Made her boyfriend most alerty,
She was voted in Bizerte
"Miss Latrine" for nineteen-thirty.

—Pvt. William L. Russell

THE FRANC

If there's anything more exasperating to the average
    Yank
It's trying to understand the value of the shifty franc
One day they push it up, the next day they drop her
So you never know if you're a millionaire or just a
    pauper
Besides, all franc notes are either torn or pasted
Together in the middle and half your time is wasted
Matching pieces. Maybe it's because the French have
    awful temperaments. And like their money full of rips
    and tears and rents. But what the hell, my francs are
    always spent
So I'll still believe a franc is just one cent!

—S/Sgt. John Willig

TO HIDE A LOVE

Can I forget
You carved your name across my lonely heart?
The vows and promises that we would never part,
The days and hours we passed with idle talk;
Your smile, your voice, the swagger in your walk.

—Lt. Sue Levins, Army Nurse Corps

HOMECOMING

I hope I'll be home again
When autumn kisses summer green
And turns it soft and brown
Like your hair in the lamplight
Of a quiet evening
To see again the winter mantle
Turn the city white and clean
And watch the kids go bellywhopping
Down the big hill in the park
To feel again my feet in civvy shoes
Slap the clean hard asphalt
Of the city streets
To see you again
Across the table in the morning
To know again
The taste of life warm and rich
And soft arms
And a bosom to take my troubles to
When I want to be a little boy again.

—Pfc. Harry Olive

★ ★ ★

WHAT IS WAR?

What is war? Some day your child may ask:
What is war? A question indeed to force you from
your appointed task
Well, I'll tell you now and you may well remember
War is battle, blood and toil
War is death on a foreign soil
War is meant to beat the Axis
War was described by a General named Sherman

—T/Sgt. Ralph B. Steiner

★ ★ ★

My first writing assignment was to be coauthor of a sports column with Sgt. David Golding and Lt. James A. Burchard. Jim decided to run our photographs smoking cigars on top of the column, to show our importance. The column was called "The Commissioners Say."

The sports page was a real hometown touch. We reported the major league baseball games and the World Series, college football scores, and the results of some of the other sporting events that we obtained from the wire services.

I had far more knowledge about sports than about war reporting because I had been a college sports editor and also had written some freelance pieces as a stringer for the *Brooklyn Eagle*. Naturally, as a Brooklyn boy, I rooted for the Brooklyn Dodgers.

Burchard, Golding, and I were given official appointments from the Algerian government, which assigned us the title of boxing commissioners.

Boxing was regulated and taken very seriously in France (Algeria was a French department, not simply a colony) and in the French army. Because Allied boxing matches took place between

American and French soldiers, the government decided that in fairness the United States should be represented on the boxing commission. Our unpaid job was to supervise the matches, weigh-ins, referees, and judges. We enjoyed the title and called each other "Commish," but we didn't take our roles too seriously.

Boxing was no big deal in the draftee American army, but it was very much a part of the rigorous French military training. The Free French had several professionals in their ranks, including Marcel Cerdan, a European champion with a long record of knockouts. Cerdan was equally well known as the boyfriend of the great Parisian chanteuse, Edith Piaf, who was nicknamed "the little sparrow."

It was tough to find a qualified American opponent to go into the ring with Cerdan and, knowing the outcome in advance, we U.S. commissioners didn't try. Instead, Cerdan was matched against other French fighters and flattened them quickly.

The knowledgeable civilian spectators, who paid to watch the fights, screamed "Box! Box!" at the fighters, which always sounded like "Bux! Bux!" to my ears. They wanted the fights to last longer and show ring skills rather than quick knockouts.

Burchard, Golding, and I took turns writing "The Commissioners Say." I always tried to write about professional American athletes in uniform. Here is one of my columns about some forgotten names today—forgotten except to baseball fans and record keepers.

THE COMMISSIONERS SAY

By Sgt. Herbert Mitgang

Judge Kenesaw Mountain Landis is getting old. So is Ford Frick. So is William Harridge. In the sports boom that is certain to follow the war, the baseball world may be looking around for a new high commissioner and new league presidents. There are few qualified figures in the States now who could become high commissioner. But there's an Army corporal in Oran, Algeria, who we think might fill the bill.

Sure, he can't speak such verra good language but he's trying the best he will. In his own rampantly efficient way, he's the czar of North African baseball, controlling more baseball players than the venerable judge. Sports writers in the States used to call him "Bananas." Here, he's called Cpl. Zeke Bonura, Army Serial Number 34078409, or just plain "Zeke" to the boys. He even lets generals call him by his first name.

When Zeke needed some bulldozers to lay out baseball diamonds, he found himself enmeshed in more red tape than you can shake a Louisville slugger at. So he confronted an American General.

"Tell him that Cpl. Zeke Bonura wants to see him about getting some bulldozers to fix up the athaletic fields," he told a colonel.

The General was busy. A half-hour later, the General was ready to see him. Zeke returned to the office. The General and his chief of staff came out to see Zeke while colonels and majors looked on, amazed.

"Hiya, General," said Cpl. Bonura.

"Hello, Zeke," said the General. "What can I do for you?"

Zeke, his two chevrons neoned against his khaki shirt, said, "It's this way. I got the fields for my boys to play on but they need sum straightened out."

The following day, he got his bulldozers.

Another day, he was teaching the British how to play baseball. A British colonel was so impressed that he invited Zeke to come to England after the war to teach the British soldiers the finer points of the game.

Zeke thinks it's a good idea. Zeke, you see, is an internationalist. He thinks some British baseball teams can be started so that a world series could truly cover the world.

"If we could have sum more international athaletics, it would be a great thing for international relations and for athaletics. The British have to learn to swing different than they do in that funny game of theirs called cricket."

Zeke knows about hitting. His lifetime batting average was .321 and one year he hit .347 for the Chicago White Sox. And despite what sports writers said about his fielding, the New Orleans banana-buster's record shows that he led the American League in fielding in 1937 and 1938.

When he first entered the Army, training camps all over the States wanted him to remain at their posts but Zeke was determined to go overseas. No bush league camps for him. He said he wanted to play in the big leagues in North Africa. So he wound up running about 150 teams for Special Services and controlling the destinies of 1,000 GI players.

Out of curiosity on a couple of Sundays—realizing that I didn't care to return here as a tourist after the war—I strolled around Algiers because it was such an exotic-looking city: a mixture of ancient Moorish and modern French architecture. (Algeria is now a forbidden country for Americans.) Algiers reminded me of San Francisco, descending from dimpled hills to a curving waterfront. Off the Boulevard de la Republique stood a major opera house and several movie houses featuring Hollywood films dubbed into French. The city was divided into different quarters and criss-crossed by palm-fringed boulevards.

One quarter, behind the stately Eglise St. Croix, was posted OFF LIMITS—the Casbah. It was considered dangerous to enter this Arab quarter, a series of dark and sullen alleyways, where men and women invited you to trade your equipment and shoes or to sell you something, including themselves.

One of my most memorable days in Algiers was July 14, 1943—
Bastille Day. An invitation came from Gen. de Gaulle's Free
French headquarters to *Stars and Stripes* to observe the celebration in the reviewing stand. Neville gave me the official pass so I
could attend. I stood a few feet away from Gen. de Gaulle on the
Rue Michelet, the main boulevard, as he saluted his few hundred marching troops. His men wore ragtag uniforms, half-colo-
nial and half-American. In the parade there were more horses
than armored vehicles, and the animals looked to be in better
shape than the half-tracks. Yet de Gaulle—aware that the eyes of
the Allies, the quixotic Arabs, and the French here and in
German-occupied France were upon him—acted as if he was
saluting a grand victorious army on the Champs-Elysees.

In my eyes, de Gaulle seemed to stand seven feet tall that day.
The Nazis and French traitors ruled his nation; the hateful Vichy
government despised him. A liberated and independent French
republic existed only in his imagination. Because of his constant
demands for recognition, he was a thorn to Roosevelt and to
Churchill, who said, "The worst cross I have to bear is the Cross
of Lorraine." (The Cross of Lorraine was the Free French symbol.)

But on that Bastille Day in wartime Algiers, I felt that Gen.
de Gaulle was a great moral force.

★ ★ ★

Our newsroom became a magnet for celebrated civilian correspondents—including Ernie Pyle, the most popular frontline
reporter with American readers, whose column we occasionally
reprinted—and various authors in uniform who loved the con-
genial stateside atmosphere.

Pvt. Irwin Shaw, the *New Yorker* short-story writer ("Girls in
Their Summer Dresses") and postwar novelist (*The Young Lions*)

drove all the way from Cairo to Algiers to see us put out the paper and say hello to old friends. Master Sgt. Dave Golding, our managing editor, invited him to write for the paper. His piece turned out to be semi-fictional. It didn't land him a job on the paper, probably because he had too big a name as a fiction writer, Dave Golding guessed.

THE DAY THE WAR ENDS

By Pvt. Irwin Shaw

There's been a lot of thought lavished on the postwar period by thought-lavishers in the highest positions, but no problem has received as much attention as how the world is going to spend the first day of the postwar period, the day of surrender. There's been a lot of speculation on this question, but so far the Army has been too busy to go into it.

It's going to start slowly. At first the men're going to climb out of the foxholes, brushing the mud off a little and just look-ing around, ready to duck back fast, in case it's all a gag. Then it's going to sink in suddenly and the Army'll start for town. The Army'll start for Paris and Bizerte, and London and Minsk, for Tripoli and Berlin, for Kansas City and Calcutta, for Yokahama and Archangel, Belfast, Cologne, Peking, and Brooklyn.

The beer will run out in the first hour and there will be fran-tic calls to Milwaukee and Munich, but the vats there will have been emptied in twenty minutes by the nearest armored divisions.

Every woman on all the seven continents between the age of ten and ninety, not under armed guard, will be kissed by an American before sunset.

By six o'clock in the evening there will be no more whiskey and the Army will go seriously into the wine period.

By six-thirty, arguments about who won the war will have begun, and 2,500 Americans, Chinese, British, Australians,

Russians, French, Greeks, Czechs, and Cubans will be under treatment for shock and contusions.

The MPs will have mysteriously disappeared from the streets and will be discovered three days later huddling in air raid shelters.

Fifteen Americans led by a corporal will be driven up to Berchtesgarden in an amphibious jeep, ropes in hand, only to find that ten million Germans had assembled there in an orderly manner and cut A. Hitler into ten million exactly equal parts.

Three thousand P-38 pilots will solemnly swear at seven o'clock never to travel on anything more rapid than the Long Island Rail Road and never to go up more than three stories in any building.

At dusk a party of soldiers will be seen off the coast of North Africa on a raft made of barrels, sailing strongly toward Hoboken.

Eleven hundred and fifteen soldiers on the verge of marriage to native girls will decide they can hold out for another couple of years and say, "Let's not do anything rash," in French, Arabic, Chinese, and Hindustani.

Second lieutenants will suddenly become very polite to privates from their hometowns whose fathers own good businesses there.

An unspecified number of top sergeants will tear off their stripes so that they can join in the singing at the bars without fear of death.

Three Arabs will wash in celebration and their wives will not recognize them and one will be bitten by his own dog.

In a park in Munich, a young lance corporal who was thought to be crazy will get up on a soapbox and declare that the German Army was never really beaten, it was betrayed from behind by a large number of Eskimos who had wormed their way into key positions in the German government. The listeners will applaud wildly.

By eleven o'clock the next morning all the aspirin will be gone.

(Pvt. Shaw wrote a piece for *The New Yorker* about an unnamed managing editor of an Army paper in Algiers as it went to press—he was, of course, Dave Golding, a fellow Brooklynite—who dreamed of getting some good rewritemen on his staff.)

To make us feel as if we were working in a regular newsroom back home, the reporters and editors sat around a large, circular copydesk, with the managing and news editors in the slot.

But the most important human touch was our copyboy—Moussi Ali, a bright ten-year-old Arab shoeshine boy, who adopted us and knew all of our names.

When we yelled "Copy!" Moussi sprang to his feet and came running. Then he carried our pencil-edited stories to the composing room where they were set in type by our GI printers.

Moussi Ali's favorite among us was Sgt. Gregor Duncan, who taught him to write his name in English. Moussi sat for hours at a typewriter, pecking out "MOUSSI ALI" hundreds of times.

When Gregor Duncan was killed on the Anzio beachhead in Italy, Moussi was inconsolable. At the mention of Greg's name, he cried and cried.

Algiers was not necessarily the safest place in embattled North Africa. Every other night, the German Luftwaffe flew across the Mediterranean from nearby Spanish airbases to bomb the ships in the harbor and the supplies on the docks. Despite claims to the contrary, Franco's Spain was not neutral during the Second World War; the Fascist dictator was paying back Nazi Germany for Hitler's help during the Spanish Civil War. (It was Hermann Goering's Luftwaffe that bombed Guernica, killing thousands of Spanish civilians.)

Bombs and shrapnel descended all over Algiers and set the streets and houses ablaze. No difference existed between military and civilian targets.

When the German bombers appeared overhead and the sirens screamed, some of us foolishly stood on the roof of our building instead of heading for the air raid shelters below. We wanted to watch the show between our anti-aircraft gunners and the Luftwaffe bombers.

One lucky night, I saw our gunners make a direct hit on a bomber. It turned into a blazing inferno. My companions and I cheered as the bomber spiraled downward and pieces of its wings and fuselage separated and fell into the water and onto the city's rooftops. Fortunately, it missed ours.

The enemy bomber carried a crew of at least five men—members of Hitler's so-called Master Race. One white parachute emerged from the burning plane and hit the ground not far from where we were watching. I doubt that the 'chutist survived the impact. The other crew members were burned alive inside the bomber's broken shell.

As I now relive that inferno in the skies more than a half-century later, I vividly remember how happy my friends and I were to see the Luftwaffe bomber ablaze.

A palpable hit! One for our side!

The horror of enemy human beings being incinerated did not trouble me at all.

At that moment, early in World War II, I did not yet know the full extent of Hitler's death camps that were systematically gassing and incinerating innocent Jewish men, women, and children in Auschwitz and in other concentration camps.

★ CHAPTER 5 ★

Algiers and Oran

"Sgt. Mitgang Decides . . ."

I F YOU INTERVIEWED a GI, regardless of age, color, or rank, about the war and his dreams for the present and the future, invariably his reply would come back like a mantra.

First: "I'd love to be home with my family by Christmas."

Second: "I'd like a steady job paying a hundred dollars a week for the rest of my life."

Christmas was the magical date on the calendar. Some soldiers in the Mediterranean and European theaters of warfare saw three or four Christmases go by before returning to the States. Except in dire family emergencies, there were no home leaves. Nor telephone calls. Communication was by V-mail; hundreds of these small lightweight letters piled up on both ends, too precious to be thrown away.

After the Depression years, a hundred dollars a week seemed like a small fortune—perhaps twice what the average city job paid or a farmhand earned. Going or returning to college after the experience of military combat didn't figure; the average soldier wanted to get started working and building a normal life. The magnanimous GI Bill was yet to come. It helped to educate ex-servicemen who otherwise would not have gone to college or trade school to acquire a profession or start a small business.

The Stars and Stripes did not have an editorial opinion page. None was needed. Nearly all the staffers were on the same wavelength, and we assumed that all the American men and women in uniform for whom we wrote thought as we did. I believed in the presidency of Franklin D. Roosevelt—soldier ballots overwhelmingly favored F.D.R.—and the New Deal social legislation that helped so many families weather the Depression. And, of course, we believed in the Allied cause. The totalitarian powers—Germany, Italy, and Japan—deserved to be despised and defeated. In the struggle against these enemies of freedom and of civilized mankind, the people of the Soviet Union were fighting on their own territory against the twentieth century's warlike Huns in Nazi guise.

Now and then, I had an urge to shoot off my mouth about what we called "The Big Picture." And so I wrote this editorial on the favorable progress of the war on different battlegrounds.

"NICE GOING"

By Sgt. Herbert Mitgang

There are some of us here in North Africa who are saying that, in this summer of '43, as Sicily is invaded and the Battle of Europe is on. Maybe we don't voice it—maybe we're just thinking about it and reluctant to express our thoughts for fear that we'll be accused of being boastful or over-patriotic. We don't want to sound as if it's the old pep talk, but we in Afrique du Nord think you guys who got a toehold in Sicily are damn good.

And while we're speaking about that, we want to repeat the same thing about the men in our Army who are fighting the Japanese in Munda—and kicking the living daylights out of them—and to the men in the Russian Army who blocked the Nazi drive and took matters into their own hands around Orel, and to you in the Chinese Army who struggle endlessly—to all of us who are battling the same enemies.

It's been a pretty good week because Adolf Hitler and Benito Mussolini held another emergency meeting in Northern Italy; they weren't discussing the weather. Perhaps the best indication of our coordinated progress can be found in Nazi propaganda. There's been a lack of optimism and, instead, a frank appeal to their wavering people to "resist, resist, resist."

Without going overboard or sounding overconfident, it has been a fine week—all over. These are the happy facts in the news. We're going places and there's a reason:

We hate injustice. And we hate it enough to fight it for the cause of freedom and fair play, anywhere.

We hate discrimination. We hate it so vehemently that we will demand equal rights for all people in all things.

We hate intolerance. So intensely that we will try to stamp it out wherever it exists in the world.

We are—positively—for many things, beginning with the Four Freedoms enunciated by President Roosevelt. These weren't always lessons we were taught in classrooms. These ideals came naturally to people brought up in free countries. Some of us learned them in the city streets and some on the farms.

Even though at times the war in Russia and China and the other fronts not our own seems remote, this week somehow they were all tied together by a series of successful events.

We don't know each other well. All we know is that our ideas are pretty much united where one dictator in particular is concerned. All roads lead to Berlin and we can talk more about these things when we get there. And maybe we'll have a beer together.

Shortly after joining *Stars and Stripes* in Algiers, I was promoted to staff sergeant—one more stripe than I had when I was busted from a buck sergeant to private in the 5th Wing.

My editorial was okayed by Capt. Neville, who had a broad knowledge of domestic and foreign affairs, and by our managing editor, Master Sgt. Dave Golding, a fellow Brooklynite, who had majored in political science at the University of Wisconsin—a school he had chosen to attend because of its progressive traditions. Dave came from a newspaper background; his father, Max Golding, was the printing foreman of *The Forward*, the largest Yiddish-language daily in the United States. Before joining the Army, Dave worked for a trade paper covering the entertainment field. Because of his Hollywood connections, *Stars and Stripes* received a regular shipment of glossy "cheesecake" pictures of leggy and bosom-y starlets that delighted readers of our "Home Front" page.

Like the other editors who were desk-bound, Golding broke away from Algiers and sometimes reported from the front in Tunisia.

When Tunis was captured and the costly campaign finally ended in the first Allied victory there, Dave reported what it was like in the following dispatch.

FREEDOM COMES TO TUNIS

By Sgt. David Golding

They had waited for Tunis a long time.

So what was a traffic jam to the Tommies, to the Australians, to the New Zealanders and Indians who had chased Field Marshal Rommel 1,800 miles from El Alemain to Tunis and right out of Africa?

Or to the British First Army which had hacked its way through djebel after djebel to take the coveted port?

Or to the Frenchmen who were coming home after three long years of Axis domination?

Tunis was now in Allied hands and only a few kilometers away. No one minded the delay except perhaps the perspiring Military Police who kept scooting up and down the road like motorcycle cops to ease the flow of traffic.

Everyone was in gay spirits, including one MP who yelled at us for attempting to nose out of line. "Keep in a bloody straight line from here to Berlin," he shouted.

The holiday spirit seemed to affect the enemy prisoners, too. As we passed the barbed-wire prison cage, we heard music. There was a band playing. It was a German infantry band the British had rounded up, instruments and all.

You couldn't help catching the spirit of a victorious army on the march. But it was nothing to what happened when we hit Tunis. It was like running into a powder keg of human emotions. When the British entered the day before, they set the spark off to one wild jamboree of exultation. The French tricolor came out of hiding. Slogans praising the British and Americans were scrawled on the white walls. The streets were filled with men, women, and children who cheered every car. They threw flowers at us and gave the V-for-Victory sign wildly.

The Brits soon taught the Yanks some of their popular barracks ballads. My favorite was "Bless 'em All."

"Bless 'em all, bless 'em all,
The long and the short and the tall
Bless all the lieutenants and WO-1s
Bless all the sergeants and their bloody sons."
There'll be no promotion,
This side of the ocean
So cheer up, my lads,
Bless 'em all!"

As wine and beer flowed, a familiar four-letter Anglo-Saxon word used in both armies replaced the word "bless."

Our combat correspondents—Sgts. Jack Foisie, Ralph G. Martin, Milton Lehman, Stanley Swinton, Paul Green, and combat photographer, Sgt. Phil Stern—attached themselves to the infantry divisions in the field. They filed long feature stories almost every day. In addition, they sent along short pieces about the human side of the war, with lots of names and hometowns, for a joint column called "Flashes from the Front." Generals and other high-ranking officers seldom made it into the column, which frequently reported amusing encounters with civilians.

To be sure, when Gen. Eisenhower got his well-deserved fourth star in February 1943, it made front-page news in *Stars and Stripes.*

Fortunately, Sgt. William Estoff was in charge of circulation. Big Bill was a B.T.O. (Big Time Operator). He used every means of transportation—planes, trucks, and even pack mules—to deliver the newspaper to faraway units in the field, on ships, and at airfields.

Sgt. Estoff had joined *Stars and Stripes* because of a lucky mistake. He was in a repple depple (replacement depot) in

England when a request came from Algiers for someone with newspaper experience. Bill, a quick-witted law-school graduate, had made a living as a bookie in Syracuse during the waning Depression years. He had truthfully written on his personnel record that he was a "bookmaker" in civilian life.

As Big Bill loved to tell the story, "Some dumb looey in the repple-depple figured that a bookmaker made books and that books and newspapers required the same skills. I didn't tell him otherwise. So I got transferred to *Stars and Stripes* instead of to some infantry outfit, which is why I'm here to tell the tale. I learned how to be the circulation manager on the job—like the rest of you guys who claimed you once used to be hotshot reporters."

To ensure that the armed forces would be covered everywhere in North Africa, Col. White and Capt. Neville decided to start other daily editions, including local news, beyond the main daily and weekly in Algiers. The first one was printed in Oran, a busy port city without the charm of Algiers, that served as an Allied naval base. Oran also had a large military hospital.

One late June day in 1943, Capt. Neville asked me to do him a favor: "Herb, take over as managing editor of the Oran edition and straighten out that bunch of amateurs."

Bob said that the dumb corporal who temporarily was serving as managing editor had screwed up—he had actually printed an anti-Semitic letter written by a French civilian in the paper's "Mail Call" column, which was reserved for our troops.

Complaints reached the Free French and Allied Force Headquarters in Algiers—it almost caused an international incident that harmed the credibility of *Stars and Stripes*.

That night, I drove a jeep westward across the Atlas Mountains, passing dramatic gorges and nomadic tribesmen mounted on camels while their bare-footed women walked behind them, to the editorial and circulation office at 6 Rue Hotel de Ville, where the paper was printed on the presses of *L'Echo d'Oran*. I was greeted with a salute by the officer in charge, a second lieutenant assigned to the Oran edition, who had no newspaper background.

When the next day's edition rolled off the presses, I noticed that our paper had a yellow look while *L'Echo d'Oran* was a clean-looking white. I immediately suspected that the French were stealing our imported American newsprint and substituting their cheap paper. Checking the pressroom the following night, my suspicions proved to be true.

I immediately reported my findings to Col. White in Algiers. He flew down to Oran the next day, reprimanded the French publisher, and told him in my presence that if our newsprint was ever stolen again, he would be reported to Gen. de Gaulle and the Free French gendarmes and jailed as a traitor. That ended the stolen newsprint affair.

Col. White then called a meeting of the entire *Stars and Stripes* staff. He introduced me as the new managing editor. The naive lieutenant serving as officer in charge piped up that he could arrange for a weekly chaplain's column. Col. White looked toward me as I grimaced.

"There will be no religion column in this newspaper," he declared. "Only Sgt. Mitgang decides what gets printed in the Oran edition. Don't even make any suggestions to him or anyone else, lieutenant. Your only job is to see that the men are well-fed, provide jeeps and trucks to cover stories and distribute the paper, and censor the mail."

Shortly thereafter, both the lieutenant and the former managing editor were kicked off *Stars and Stripes* and shipped to a repple depple.

Shaping up the Oran edition required me to do most of the writing and editing. Once again, I introduced a column of news about the United States called the "Home Front." And I built up the sports page, picking up pieces as often as possible by Lt. Jim Burchard, who knew more than any of us about sports. During the World Series, Jim contributed a poem to the paper.

WARTIME SERIES—BATTER UP

By Lt. Jim Burchard

The airman climbs into his ship, and speeds toward Axis land,
He drops his load of calling cards, with cool and practiced
hand.
But as the bombs crash far below, on railroads, guns, and tanks,
The airman's thoughts are far away, he's doping out the Yanks.
A sailor on an LCT is blasted off the deck,
He flops into the water from a twisted, flaming wreck.
This doughty tar went under twice, yes, he was damn near
drowned,
He murmured, as he slid below, "Will Chandler take the
mound?"
The grimy doughboy crawls along a hillside raked by shells,
Big German guns have made his world the hottest of all hells.
But as he races to the charge, what does the doughboy do?
He hollers at a buddy, "Fifty bucks on St. Loo."

I also reprinted material from the Algiers edition that Capt. Neville, with his great knowledge of foreign affairs and interest in the postwar world, emphasized. This serious stuff was not the kind of news found in the average hometown newspaper, but I too believed that *Stars and Stripes* had an educational role to play—and that we could improve upon the gossip that passed for news in the American tabloid press.

The following roundup of opinions ran on our masthead page in one issue of the Oran edition.

THE PEACE TABLE

The "battle for peace" after our Allied victory is being considered at the same moment that our armed forces are engaged in military battles on the land, seas, and in the skies. Opinions naturally vary on the details, but there is agreement that the time to plan for peace is now. Here are some recent quotations on the subject:

Vice President Henry A. Wallace: "In a world free from misery, the peoples will fraternize and frontiers will lose their importance."

Mme. Chiang Kai-Shek: "We are all engaged in a combined effort, from which will emerge a new world, wherein mankind everywhere may enjoy the permanent fruits of prosperity."

William C. Bullitt, former ambassador to Russia and France: "A European Federation, providing a strong, integrated, democratic Europe is necessary to peace. The people of the United States Government will not underwrite tyranny imposed on people by any other people, nor will they insure or guarantee slavery."

Colonel Knox, Secretary of the Navy: "America is now discussing with New Zealand the postwar ownership of the American airbase on the island of Upulu in the Samoan area of the South Pacific. We are not grabbing anything, but

America should discuss with other powers to the end that we will possess permanent military bases where needed for future protection."

Sumner Welles, Under-Secretary of State: "America will press for a United Nations conference to clear up clashing policies in international economics. If we don't make a start now there is danger that we shall be brought to peace with as many plans as there are governments."

I was grateful for Col. White's words to the whole staff in Oran. His words proved, once again, that *Stars and Stripes* was mainly run by and for enlisted men.

CHAPTER 6

Palermo I

Do You Speak Sicilian?

WHEN SICILY was invaded in the summer of 1943, it signaled that the battle for Europe was finally being waged on enemy territory—the largest island in the Mediterranean. The American 7th Army, led by Lt. Gen. George S. Patton, Jr., fought its way up the western side and captured the capital city of Palermo, while the seasoned British 8th Army, led by Gen. Sir Bernard Law Montgomery, slogged its way toward Messina on the northeastern side.

After thirty-nine days of hard fighting in the rugged mountain terrain against German and Italian troops, the victorious Allied forces conquered the island.

Everyone on *The Stars and Stripes* staff in North Africa wanted to leave behind the "A-rabs," whom we did not trust and whose culture few of us understood, and live closer to the more familiar Europeans, whose ancestry resembled our own.

And, if we remembered our literature, we wanted to see the mythical Greek places of Sicily. I was fascinated by the fact that the Allies were now on the land and along the littoral of Homer's *Odyssey*.

While the fighting was still in progress, a new edition of the newspaper was published on the presses of the Giornale di Sicilia, on Piazza Giulio Cesare, near the railroad station in Palermo. The first few issues were staffed by several of the experienced correspondents and editors—Sgts. Jack Foisie, Ralph G. Martin, William Hogan, and Stanley Meltzoff, an artist who did our illustrations. Master Sgt. Irv Levinson came over from Algiers to check out the printing facilities. The officer in charge was Lt. Jim Burchard, my fellow boxing commissioner in Algiers. Jim told us that when he interviewed enlisted men for a story, he had to take off his bars so they would speak more freely; for that reason, he cautioned us against being made commissioned officers if we wanted to remain free-ranging reporters.

After downing his daily carafe of vino, Jim Burchard frequently repeated his favorite tale: how *Stars and Stripes* came to be published at the Giornale di Sicilia.

> I walked into the office of Signor Ardizzone, the publisher, gave him the old "buon giorno" and told him that we wanted to print the American Army newspaper in his plant. When he hesitated, I patted my holster and shoved a fresh clip into my .45. He got the point right away. We agreed on the deal— *Stars and Stripes* would supply its own newsprint and ink and our GI printers would have the use of his Linotype machines and presses.
>
> No argument—after all, our boys beat the Nazis and Fascists and freed Palermo, right? Right! Since Virginia tobacco

wasn't available in Sicily, I sweetened the deal by bringing him a couple of cartons of Camels. Cigarettes were the best currency in Sicily—with a few packs of butts, you could buy anything from a hand-painted cart to a fancy coffin.

Later Signor Ardizzone and I became good friends and he told me how proud he was to publish such a fine-looking American newspaper now that Mussolini's Roman stooges had been kicked out of Sicily. He said that before everything that was printed in his plant—even a wedding announcement—had to be licensed by Mussolini's Fascists.

Now, it was "finito Benito!" time in Sicily. So up yours, Benito!

After I shaped up the Oran edition, Capt. Neville ordered me to go to Palermo and take over as managing editor of the Sicily edition.

There, I made it a policy for the deskmen to get out and do some writing; a byline was good for any newsman's morale. Bill Hogan, the *San Francisco Chronicle* literary critic and editor, wrote a light-hearted piece on a hometown subject.

SHAVE AND A HAIRCUT—IN SICILY

By Sgt. William Hogan

Like many another GI, I am fascinated by the glitter of Italian barbershops, the interiors of which generally are as vivid and rich as the mixing shelf in an uptown bar. I find the places pleasant and relaxing, and after some preliminary fussing with your scalp by one of a half-dozen energetic and cooperative operators, you are left alone for a while—the way it should happen in any tonsorial parlor. Indeed, you are invited to think or read or sleep or dream as you please.

An establishment for the care of the hair called "Nick's English Spoken" was mine alone one afternoon. Alone, that is, until a white-clad Italian nudged me slightly and said out of the side of his mouth:

"You from Hollywood, Bud?"

This apparently was Nick, with the English spoken.

Another barber stood alongside him. I grunted, shifted my position, and looked at them. Out of the side of my mouth I replied:

"What makes you think so?"

"The haircut," he said. "Strictly from the Boulevard. Used to cut 'em like that out there myself."

The hair was a style caused only by not having had much contact with places like "Nick's English Spoken" for a number of weeks.

I told Nick I was not from Hollywood, and he turned to the second barber.

"Okay," he said, in English. "You win. We have our little bets." He turned to me. "He's from Perth Amboy. Jersey. I used to work all over—Missoula, Duluth, Los Angeles. Ever been to those places?"

"Can't say I have," I said.

"You might wonder at the excellence of barber shops in Italy," Nick said. "It is really a combination of shops in the United States, where most Italian barbers receive their apprenticeship. And it is also a source of little bets."

"We can tell the origin of our American customers," the second barber said. "Hair cutting is a matter of geography, more than of age, personality, or good looks. It is a matter of climatic zones and the state of one's nerves."

"Bets run about fifty-fifty," Nick said. "Where you from?"

"Me? From San Francisco," I informed the proprietor.

"Never been there." He turned to his co-worker and betting companion. "Ever been to Frisco, Guido?"

Guido, with regret, shook his head.

I turned to Nick. "Do all Italian barbers who come to America in the interest of the trade travel as much as you do?"

"Oh, sure," Nick said. "The best places and the worst places. It is the apprenticeship for the barbershops of excellence in Italy."

"You might say it is in the interest of research," said the second barber, who used to work in Perth Amboy, Jersey.

"On your bill from me, please add another pack of Lucky Strikes."

Nick carefully looked me over with a frown. "Strictly from Beverly Boulevard," he said. "But then, of course, we've never been to Frisco."

"Egg shampoo?" Guido asked

I had come too long a way from home to have my first egg shampoo in "Nick's English Spoken," and told him no, no egg shampoo.

It's not the way in San Francisco.

To show our loyal GI audience that *Stars and Stripes* would be as much pleasure to read in Sicily as in North Africa, we also ran "cheesecake"—one of the first was perhaps the sexiest picture to come out of Hollywood during the war. It showed Betty Grable in a tight-fitting bathing suit looking over one shoulder while, below, the well-rounded cheeks of her behind smiled in the reader's face.

As a service to the troops, we also began to print Italian lessons—the cause of my first trouble in Sicily.

The lessons were called "Parlate Italiano?" (Do you speak Italian?). We wanted to teach more than what the GIs called "shooting the old buon giorno."

The good deed quickly got me into hot water.

One of the clowns on my staff who helped prepare the lessons decided to jazz them up. He included such phrases as: "In America, I am a millionaire." That was amusing and possibly practical if trying to make out with a signorina.

Then one day this phrase appeared: "My beard is two feet long."

An angry delegation of Sicilian men and women who worked as translators for the Allied Military Government showed up at my desk in the Giornale di Sicilia, breathing fire. First, they told me that young people in Palermo used the language lessons in reverse—to learn English. Next, they informed me that we had printed an obscene phrase.

Didn't I know that "My beard is two feet long" was a sexual boast that also could refer to another part of the male anatomy?

I was shocked, pleaded innocence, and apologized on behalf of the United States of America and President Franklin Delano Roosevelt.

Thereafter, I made sure that a professor of languages at the University of Palermo checked Parlate Italiano? before the lessons were set into type.

The next crisis was partly of my own making. It concerned none other than Gen. George Patton, whose 7th Army headquarters were based in Palermo.

The rumor that he had slapped a wounded soldier in a hospital in Sicily, supposedly for malingering, turned out to be true. Actually, the soldier was suffering from battle fatigue.

The news was broken in the American press. We received newspaper clippings from home about the incident; so did many GIs.

I thought that *Stars and Stripes* ought to print the facts. Otherwise, we could be accused of suppressing known news. I knew it was sensitive so I decided not to run our own story—instead, we would simply reprint an Associated Press dispatch and bury it on an inside page.

Before doing so, I asked Lt. Jim Burchard for his advice.

"If we run the piece here in 7th Army country, and General Patton reads it and throws up his breakfast, we'll both be on permanent KP for the rest of this war," Jim counseled.

I pleaded that for the paper's integrity, we ought to have it on record that we tried.

"Let them censor it—not us," I foolishly reasoned.

Which is exactly what the censor, a scared 7th Army public relations major, did when I showed him the page proofs. I didn't bother to challenge him—he looked too frightened before giving me a dirty look and killing the Patton piece.

"Let Ike handle Georgie," the P.R. major confided. "Do you wise guys on *Stars and Stripes* want to make things worse for all of us here? Don't forget, you're in the Army too."

I beat a hasty retreat to the Giornale composing room and killed the AP dispatch. That ended what became a well-known Patton story that had given Gen. Eisenhower—who ordered his tough general to apologize to the hospital staff—a headache. Nevertheless, Ike needed Patton to command an army in northern France after D-Day.

That was one of the rare times that one of our stories was censored.

To fill the news hole left by the censored piece, I ran one of Ernie Pyle's standby columns. Ernie, a good friend of *Stars and Stripes*, was the most popular American correspondent with readers in the States. I had first met him in Algiers, after the end of the Tunisian campaign, when he dropped into our newsroom during a rainstorm, shivering wet, hungry, and looking much too skinny. Like our own combat correspondents, Ernie glorified the fighting men; we often ran his very human columns.

A fortunate addition to *Stars and Stripes* was Bill Mauldin, the greatest soldier-cartoonist to come out of World War II, or any other American war, whose "Up Front . . . By Mauldin" drawing ran on the upper right-hand corner of our masthead page. His detailed drawings and perfect captions featured Willie and Joe, two bearded riflemen. They didn't simply tell jokes; they commented on battlefield life as experienced by enlisted men.

Originally, Sgt. Mauldin drew for the *45th Division News*, where his talent was first spotted by *Stars and Stripes* combat correspondents. One afternoon, he turned up in our office at the Giornale di Sicilia. Our staff artist, Sgt. Stanley Meltzoff, a painter and art teacher, looked at Mauldin's work and immediately said, "He's the first American Army cartoonist whose drawings remind me of the famous British cartoonist, Bruce Bairnsfather, who drew a strip called 'The Better 'Ole' during the First World War. This guy Mauldin's better than Bairnsfather or any American military artist anywhere. His characters have the looks and voices of real frontline GIs. We ought to run his stuff in *Stars and Stripes*."

Bill Mauldin had come to see us not for a job on *Stripes* but to obtain zinc for his own "cuts" (engravings) in the *45th Division News*. Zinc was in short supply during the war. For that reason, Jim Burchard and I had gone around to the funeral parlors in Palermo and bought up all their surplus zinc for our artists' "cuts." In Sicily, where a funeral was a colorful event with music and caparisoned horses leading the mourners, zinc was used to line the coffins of the deceased.

Eventually, Bill Mauldin joined *Stars and Stripes* in Naples. Ernie Pyle wrote a column about "Up Front . . . By Mauldin," which added to his growing fame. The independent Mauldin would drive his jeep to the 5th Army frontlines in Italy, gather ideas, then draw a batch of his daily cartoons.

Once in a great while, he would show me a rough draft of a drawing after he had joined *Stars and Stripes*. Sometimes I would offer a suggestion—which he wisely rejected—about adding an "and" or a "but" to a caption. Mauldin's ear was pitch-perfect about the way that Willie and Joe spoke.

Bill won his first Pulitzer Prize for his brilliant drawings from *Stripes* that appear in his essential book, *Up Front*. It has been reprinted many times and remains on every wartime bookshelf to this day. After the war, as an editorial cartoonist for the *St. Louis Post-Dispatch*, he won another Pulitzer.

More good luck for *Stripes* arrived in the person of Lt. (j.g.) William Brinkley, who was stationed on a destroyer that was berthed in Palermo harbor.

Bill Brinkley appeared at our office in the Giornale di Sicilia, announced that he was a writer, and offered to report about the role played by the U. S. Navy in supporting invasions, chasing enemy U-boats, and about Allied shipboard life. After reading his stylish pieces, we quickly piped him aboard *Stars and Stripes*.

He became the *Stars and Stripes* naval correspondent, adding to our floating readership.

YANK AT SEA

By Lt. (j.g.) Bill Brinkley

The Mediterranean is no kind mistress these days to the men who would woo her.

Out of the north and east the squally, angry winds scream of approaching winter. The "Med," as men of the Navy call her, loses her summer blue for a chilling black with a breast of snowy whitecaps. Cold, stinging waves crash over a ship's dipping decks.

Tonight I am writing these lines in a shaking hand below decks of a small British craft which has been scouting these waters for German surface shipping.

The whirling electric fan has just tumbled on the head of the man in front of me. The table is sliding from one side of the compartment to the other. Just now two dishes fly off a ledge and crash into a thousand pieces against the bulkhead.

The sort of sea and weather that test a man's guts down to the last tendril are now setting in for a stay of months. It's a good Navy man who can keep his chow down tonight. Topside the men are doing a hell of a lot more. Out where the devil's elements are on a spree they're spitting back defiance. They're standing on open decks against rain, against everything the maddened Med can throw at them.

A man who has just been relieved on the after-gun watch comes dripping in, shedding his wet black raincoat and shaking himself like a drenched dog. He is a peacetime landlubber made into a real warring seaman. His kind are the fiber of any Navy in wartime. This particular man was doing a loom job in a cotton mill before war came.

"God, what a bloody sea," he is saying, running a hand through a heavy black beard. "Worst we've had since last year. I wonder who the bloke was who called this the calm blue Mediterranean."

Out of the east a wet wind whines across the deck and for a moment is silent. From the black sky a low threatening rumble begins to cut its way through the fierce dissonance of the sea. The rumble becomes a mighty roar. Suddenly a hideous scar splits the sky. In the hanging moment of lightning-bright the shrouded faces of the gunners stand out sharp and tense.

Needling rain beats across them. The thunder is gone, spent. The sea screams on triumphantly.

The Med is getting tougher than tough. But the faces of the men do not flinch.

After completing his shipboard duties, Bill Brinkley returned to the *Stars and Stripes* office almost every night, found a quiet corner, and began writing a novel. After the war, his *Don't Go Near the Water* was published to great acclaim.

I wanted our readers to be aware that Sicily was full of historical and architectural treasures that they could explore on their off-days and write home about. We printed the locations of museums, churches, and palaces; most of them had survived the bombings, although their facades were nicked here and there. For sightseeing in Palermo, we recommended the Palazzo Reale, the gaudiest palace in Sicily, home of kings since the 12th century.

For the fun of it, Lt. Jim Burchard, the seasoned sports writer; Sgt. Stanley Meltzoff, our staff artist; and I, the managing editor and a new lawyer, did joint articles about the Palazzo Reale from our own professional perspectives—for our own amusement more than for the enlightenment of our readers and our Sicilian friends who read *Stars and Stripes*.

THE ROYAL PALACE—THREE SOLDIERS' VIEWS

By Sgt. Stanley Meltzoff, art instructor

The Royal Palace is similar to a garbage scow full of junk jewelry in which someone has hidden a black pearl. Architects have built it for 900 years on the principle that everything done before was atrocious, and generally each architect was right.

The Saracens started the palace by hiring Sicilians to build in the manner of the Persians, and the Normans continued by employing Arabs to repair the ruins in the fashion of the Greeks. The Spaniards then tacked on a number of palatial out-houses modeled after the Neapolitan, and eventually the Italians hired an interior decorator schooled in France. The resulting complex of Islamic, Italo-Byzantine, Baroque, and Classicistic, with one exception, may be described as lousy.

The greatest part of the interior, if scraped clean of gold leaf, would occupy twelve scrapers thirty-two years and the net yield of gold would far exceed the value of the decor. Stylistically, the late 19th century decoration of the Royal Suite is a fine example of the Neo-Asinine.

Shuddering slightly, the art critic walks through this repulsive labyrinth in the hope of arriving quickly in the two chambers that contain 12th century mosaics; the Capella Palatina, or palace chapel, and the room of King Roger. These Norman mosaics preserve in forms of rigid elegance barbarism transformed into freshness aged into exoticism. Most curious is the appearance of Syrian motifs in an exceedingly well-preserved Norman work in so apparent a fashion as to document the Arabic influence. The resulting style can be called Neo-Asinine.

Lt. James A. Burchard, sportswriter

Charlie Atlas and Lionel Strongfort boast pretty fair biceps, but they should take a quick peek at an upstairs room in this palace. It's quite a spacious place, about big enough to include the Yankee Stadium and a nine-hole golf course, and decorating the walls are huge murals of an old-timer who probably could have won the Olympics single-handed.

Beside this gent, Atlas and Strongfort would look like the "before" in one of their "before and after" health posters. He hasn't got a Tommy gun or a bazooka to help him out—only a big club. But how he can swing it! The pictures show him clouting a seven-headed Hydra where it will do the most good, throttling a lion, tossing some gent named Anteus into the stratosphere, holding the world on his back, subduing Cerebrus, the three-headed guardian of Hades, with a dirty look, and several other little items of mayhem.

Personally we could go for any of his feats, except the one about holding the world while Atlas took a short break.

Anyway, it's a cinch this guy didn't eat C-rations. Red meat and probably plenty of nectar. He forgot to visit his barber, judging by the alfalfa on his noble chin, but when it comes to muscle this guy is in a class by himself.

Who is he? Why, Hercules, of course. The pictures are a story of him performing a lot of trick jobs he had to do for some king or queen. Not being up on mythology, I don't remember the exact reason. But for my dough, these pictures top the collection. Man oh man, what a fullback that guy would have made.

Sgt. Herbert Mitgang, lawyer

The Kings County courthouse in Brooklyn was never like this. All the real estate men whose offices are the nearest fire hydrant could have used these great halls, rent-free.

Old Bailey and the English common law were far superior to the palatial justice that reigned in this palazzo. For here was the divine law of kings—the most one-sided law of all, based not on *res adjudicata* but upon the current whims of one ruler clad in ermine.

I was interested to see the prison in the palace and witness the methods used to persuade untalkative prisoners. In truth, I thought I might pick up a client or two, preferably some rich old baron who was about to be hung. Yes, there is a prison but, damn, no baron, and although the bones of slow-paying clients have shriveled these long centuries, they still rattle and walk in these dungeons. The rubber-hose methods of obtaining evidence are no longer admissible in the United States, but it was the preferred method in this old prison.

Verily, the luxury of the palazzo is breathtaking and for the moment the grandeur and art works seem well worth the costly entrance fees paid by the people. But as you walk out, it is impossible not to overlook the ill-shod, poorly clad guide walking on a gilded inner court. Give the poor guy a handful of lire. He and his ancestors paid for this mess.

Almost immediately after the downfall of fascism, a warm relationship formed between the newly liberated Sicilian people and American and British soldiers. We became diplomats in khaki and olive-drab, leaving a residue of goodwill forever.

In his wise novel, *A Bell for Adano*, John Hersey, a greatly respected civilian correspondent, described the relationship idealistically. (Hersey, who later became a friend of mine through our work together in the Authors Guild, wrote about a group of Hiroshima survivors in *The New Yorker*. It was the most important magazine article of the postwar years, and awakened the world to the dangers of the atom bomb and of radiation.)

Similarly, our own lively *Stars and Stripes* correspondent, Ralph G. Martin, wrote about an actual town that was brought to life by an Allied Military Government official. (Martin later became a distinguished Churchill and presidential historian.)

DEATH AND A NEW LIFE IN A SICILY TOWN

By Sgt. Ralph G. Martin

It's a slow process, the rebirth of a dead town. The story of Marsala is the story of villages and towns and cities all over Sicily. It's the story of the work of AMG—Allied Military Government.

Marsala may be said to have died at noon on Garibaldi Day, May 11. That's when several of our big bombers swept in low from the sea, taking two hours to empty their bomb bays. When they left, Marsala looked like a squashed tomato.

There had been ample warning to the 30,000 people in this winemaking city that fronts the sea on Sicily's west coast. Allied planes had dropped thousands of leaflets and the radio had told people to get out of town.

It was two months later, on July 24, that U.S. Third Division troops marched into Marsala after some short, bitter fighting in the outskirts. Marching with them was Capt. William Jequier, an AMG captain.

"I was told to take charge of Marsala," the captain said, "but there was no Marsala. There were just bricks and litter and the smell of the dead."

At 57, the captain is a graying man with a strong, full face and a determined tone in his soft-speaking voice.

Ghosts don't fight, so the infantry boys shoved out for other places. But the captain moved into the local police, or Carabinieri, office in the immediate suburb and went to work. For four days, all alone without communications or transport, the captain shaped some order out of the chaos.

The job was doubly tough because the people were spread out as far as fifteen miles in a semi-circle around the city. But as soon as they heard the Americans had taken over, they began to dribble back.

"They all acted like a bunch of spoiled brats," said the captain. "From somewhere they got the idea that the Americans would come marching in loaded down with clothes and food and money. Some were expecting new donkey carts, cigarettes, new homes. It took a while before they woke up."

But the Sicilian "children" did understand finally. And under the captain's direction, they started to clear away the rotting dead, filling the road craters, tying together the broken bridges, pulling down the tottering lonely walls of blasted buildings.

Still the hungry had to be fed, the homeless had to be housed.

For the homeless, the 10,000 who came back, Captain Jequier requisitioned every building that still stood up plus the extra homes of the extra-wealthy in the surrounding suburbs. For food, the captain went to Trapani for three trucks, sent them out daily to buy up all the grain and corn in the area, and then ordered all the people to turn in their excess foodstuffs for the common food pool. By this time the captain no longer worked alone. The Carabinieri and the mayor were giving him fulltime cooperation. The mayor was the tallest man in town with the softest voice. He had been mayor for thirteen years and owned the biggest winery until the bombs fell. "When those bombs came," he said, "I was a mayor without a city."

When the trucks returned with the grain, there was no electric power to run the mills to make the flour. So again the captain went scrounging and came up with two old diesel engines.

These Sicilians eat simply. Some bread, spaghetti and a little wine is all most of them asked for. But for the extras, there was the black market. There, too, AMG stepped in fast. All prices were fixed, black marketeers were arrested. The captain set up a court for hearings on each case.

The police are on the lookout for other things, such as looting, kids playing ball with Italian hand grenades, fishermen going beyond the dangerous three-mile limit. And when the police got too sloppy, the captain bawled them out.

Then there are a bunch of little unexpected things that crop up, like the horse-donkey stud problem. Under the old regime, the state owned all the stud horses and donkeys and rented them out to the farmers, charging them 150 lire per service. The Sicilians didn't want any other system, so would the captain please take care of the stud farm and continue things as they were?

Then there was the girl with a baby in her belly who wanted the captain to release her boyfriend from one of our prison camps so he could come back and marry her.

There are 500 people who line up outside the captain's office every day with their problems. Some want passes to go to a different city, some want simple things like mailing a letter to the States, and there are still plenty of men who wait to tell the captain, "I am a prisoner . . . I want to surrender."

The captain himself is used to headaches. Before the war he was general manager of a large international perfumery house. He walked out of Paris the day before the Germans walked in. He was in London trying to enlist in the army for months. The British finally decided that he wasn't too old for them. Here in Sicily, he landed on D-Day and his first AMG job was in Comiso.

In Marsala today, there is a new sense of order, a new faith that the Americans will help rebuild a new Marsala out of the rubble. The people know that nobody will starve, nobody will have to sleep in the streets, nobody will be punished without a fair trial. They know, too, that anyone can go up to the Captain with their complaint or problem—a democratic fact that continually amazes them.

★ ★ ★

I was eternally fascinated by the Allied Military Government and the contrast between the American and British governors in dealing with the newly liberated people. Even before the AMG landed in Sicily, conflicts arose about how to run the defeated Axis nation. Could the AMG truly be allied? Should it be a military or civilian presence?

The White House and Downing Street disagreed. I later discovered that President Roosevelt and Prime Minister Churchill had different views of the peacetime shape of the democratic world.

Always interested in maintaining British hegemony around the Mediterranean, Churchill tried to persuade Roosevelt that the United Kingdom should rule Sicily. In a secret message to Roosevelt about Husky (the code name for the Sicily invasion), Churchill rather brazenly said:

"I hope that you may feel in view of the fact that the Force commander under the supreme direction of General Eisenhower will be British [General Sir Harold R.L.G. Alexander], with two prima donnas under him, Gen. George S. Patton and Gen. Bernard L. Montgomery, we should be senior partner in the military administration of enemy-occupied territory in that area. Our proposal will be that under the supreme authority of Gen. Eisenhower a British General officer should be appointed as Military Governor of Husky-land and that he should be assisted by a Joint Anglo-American staff. Thus there would be no dualism in actual executive decisions on the spot."

Roosevelt would not buy Churchill's demand for British domination. He reasoned:

"In view of friendly feelings toward America entertained by a great number of citizens of the United States who are of Italian descent, it is my opinion that our military problems will be made less difficult by giving to the Allied Military Government as much of an American character as is practicable.

"This can be accomplished by appointing to the offices of the Allied Military Government a large proportion of Americans."

Churchill backed down; for once, language had failed him. He explained that by "senior partner" he had meant only that there should be not two voices but one. And he added that "the two flags should always be displayed and we should present a united and unbreakable front in all directions."

The divided command set up by Roosevelt and Churchill took some of the burden off Gen. Eisenhower's shoulders. The top man for the British was Gen. Alexander, the formal military governor, and his chief civil affairs officer was Gen. Lord Rennell of Rodd, an international banker whose father had served as ambassador to Italy. Baron Rodd clearly outranked the American civil affairs chief under Gen. Patton, Lt. Col. Charles Poletti, despite the fact that Poletti had briefly served as governor of New York.

In wartime Italy, however, Poletti had one big advantage over Rodd—his name ended in a vowel, like so many family names.

The transition from fascism to democracy under AMG was a steady source of news and amusement.

I wrote about the new educational system. Under the Fascists all the textbooks were filled with propaganda and had to be replaced. Even young children learned their ABCs in the service of the dictatorship; for example, the letter M stood for both Mother and Mussolini—if you loved one, you loved the other, too.

Lt. Col. Poletti posted numerous decrees to change the traditional conduct of the Sicilians, who were disinclined to break their age-old habits. And so the people made up a little ditty about him that, in rich dialect, went:

"Charlie Poletti, Charlie Poletti,
    Let's have less Charlie,
And more spaghetti!"

Among the wisecracking officers around AMG, the Baron also
inspired a ditty that began:

"Here's to Lord Rennell of Rodd,
Whose forebears spoke only to God."

The tenor of these satirical jingles reflected one of the key differ-
ences between the two Allies' approaches to their mission. Britain
had brought centuries of experience in colonial rule; the Brits
posted orders and expected them to be obeyed. The United
States, however, born of anti-colonialism, brought mixed signals
to the task. Even as they sought progressive reform in Sicily, the
Yanks tried to effect change through more personal encounters.

Needless to say, I did not attempt to print the Poletti and
Rodd jingles in *Stars and Stripes*, knowing they would have been
censored and might cut us off from our AMG sources.

Sgt. Mitgang, managing editor of *Stars and Stripes* (Sicily), standing on a balcony of the staff's requisitioned hotel in Palermo, 1943. (Mitgang Collection)

THE STARS AND STRIPES.

THIBODAUX, LA., WEDNESDAY, MARCH 11, 1863.

The Stars and Stripes,

Is published in the City of Thibodaux, La., by the proprietors, semi-occasionally. Price—picayune per copy, ALWAYS IN ADVANCE.

HOW A MAN FEELS IN BATTLE.

There can be nothing more puzzling than the analysis of one's feelings on a battle field. You cannot describe them satisfactorily to yourself or others. To march steadily up to the mouths of a hundred cannon, while they pour out fire and smoke and shot and shell in a storm that mows the men like grass, is horrible beyond description—appalling. It is absurd to say a man can do it without fear. During Hancock's charge at Fredericksburg, for a long distance the slope was swept by such a hurricane of death that we thought every step would be our last, and I am willing to say, for one, that I was pretty badly scared. Whatever may be said about "getting used to it," old soldiers secretly dread a battle equally with new ones. But the most difficult thing to stand up under is the suspense while waiting, as we waited in Fredericksburg, drawn up in line of battle on the edge of the field, watching the columns file past us and disappear in a cloud of smoke, where horse and men and colors go down in confusion, where all sounds are lost in the screaming of shells, the cracking of musketry, the thunder of artillery, and knowing that our own turn comes next, expecting each moment the word "Forward." It brings a strange kind of relief when "Forward" comes. You move mechanically with the rest. Once fairly in for it, your sensibilities are strangely blunted—you care comparatively nothing about the sights that shocked you at first—men torn to pieces by cannon shot become a matter of course. At such a time there comes a latent sustenance from within us, which no man anticipates who has not been in such a place before, and which most men pass through without knowing anything about. Those who say they would like to visit a battle field seldom know what they are talking about. After darkness has put an end to the struggle, a hush settles over the field—such a contrast to the roar of the fight! Never is silence more oppressive, more eloquent. You hear the cries of the wounded, which are never distinguished while the work is going on. A stray shot hurtles through the darkness overhead. You hear the ambulance wheels chirr heavily along, grinding through the soil with a sullen, muffled sound, like some monster crunching the bones of his victims. You see the outline of forms gliding through the gloom, carrying on litters, pale, bloody men. You stumble over—perhaps your friend—with his hair matted in blood over his white face, and his dead eyes staring blindly up to the sky. You are startled by the yells of those lifted about, after becoming cold and stiff in their blood. Follow to the hospital, and see those whose lives clung to them on the field, dissected alive, and butchered. They writhe a few hours or days, are tumbled into a trench, their graves unknown, forgotten forever. Then talk about the horrors of war.

C. H.

Written for the Stars and Stripes.

PRINCIPLE VERSUS POLICY,

OR A WORD TO COPPERHEADS.

There has ever been a proneness in mankind to sacrifice Principle for Policy, to give up right for expediency. Yet the history of this world demonstrates conclusively that such sacrifices are almost invariably disastrous to those who thus consent to barter away for present gain the future weal of themselves, and of the unborn millions who succeed them.

Occasionally, like sun-gleams across the ocean's billows, are to be found instances, noble and heroic—of an unswerving devotion to Principle—a sublime inundation of entire peoples upon its altar, and rivers of blood shed in its defense. Such steady adherence to the cause they espoused—the success of their efforts, have rendered the ages in which they transpired epochs—and their names and nations immortal.

The English people in their gigantic contest with Napoleon I.—Our own Revolutionary Fathers in their struggle with the mother country—The "30 years' war" in Germany, waged for Civil and Religious Liberty—The bloody struggle of the Covenanters of Scotland—of the Huguenots of France; and I might go on to enumerate until History becomes beclouded in fable, but it is not necessary: the number is sufficient—they stand like beacon lights along the shore of time, beckoning to us of to-day to emulate their efforts and to imitate their example if we would be true to ourselves and false to no one that shall come after us. We as Americans, as citizens of one of the greatest republics that ever rose and raised in the development of human affairs, ought to listen to this story of heroic actions, and be ever and always true to the exigency of the hour, by preserving our national unity for ourselves and for the unborn millions who are to rise up and either bless or curse our memories, as we prove true or false to them and their liberties. We expect that rebels, who "have to hell's perdition gone," will persist in their effort to destroy our government. But equally lamentable is the fact, that there are a class of men in the North even, who as strongly persist that their efforts shall be successful. To reason with such men is folly. They worship no God but Policy. They bow at no shrine but that of Party; they know no other word but "Peace!" What though the geographical formation of this country tells us it should be one; what though our own political supremacy, interest, life tells us that it is absolutely essential to preserve its entirety; what though defeat, dark, disgraceful defeat, clings to our banner; what though the martyred dead, sleeping in their bloody fields, cry in our ears unavenged! Yet in reply to all this, to everything, we hear "Peace! Peace!" Who loves peace more than the soldier far from home, far, in far and its toys? When, on midnight, comes to cheer our pathway, our souls glad, our hearts, we will close firm and steadfast around the old flag, and, like the "Old Guard" at the battle of Waterloo, we can die for its defense, but never, never! shall in its defense. We tell the "Peace Men" of the North that, truly, that they can never control the destinies of this country as long as our swords are our own. That never, under the delusive song of Peace, shall the citizen soldiers of the republic be lulled to sleep while Freedom is bound, gagged and tossed like a cricket ball ever into the arms of Jeff. Davis and the Richmond junta. The object of our hopes is the re-establishment of Federal Authority over our whole country. For this we labor and suffer, and for this Oh! how many have died! Anything short of this is virtually sacrificing Principle to temporary expediency. Let the "stay at home" "keep silent until they can do something else besides talk. When rebellion sinks beneath the earth, then we will cry with gladsome voice Peace until then our voice is for war, aggressive, relentless war!

The air is ever more pure when the storm cloud has passed, so let us trust that when this war is all over and gone our liberties shall be more pure and precious to us and those who shall succeed us. Then we shall not have lived altogether in vain, but shall have performed our part in the great drama, that shall aid to make our age illustrious—our nation entire, our memories blessed. For this "consummation devoutly hoped for" let us learn to labor and to wait—ever the devoted champions of Principle in opposition to the seductive blandishments of policy.

A rare Civil War edition of *Stars and Stripes*, printed in 1863 in a captured Confederate plant in Louisiana by Union Army printers. (Mitgang Collection)

THE STARS AND STRIPES
AFRICA

Vol. 1, No. 33, Saturday, July 24, 1943   U. S. Army Newspaper   Two Francs

Palermo Taken As Americans Cut Across Island To North Coast

Nazi Offensive On Eastern Front Becomes Retreat

Red Army Pounding At Orel, Key Enemy Defense Base

The great German offensive on the Russian front went into reverse gear this week. Not only had the drive launched early this month by the vaunted Wehrmacht been stopped dead, but the Red Army was sweeping forward in a powerful counter attack that threw the Germans back beyond their starting positions.

By the week's end, Soviet forces were pounding at the gates of Orel, key Nazi bastion on the central front. The fury of the Russian drive marked a critical point in the Battle of Eastern Europe.

But much more significant than mere territorial gains or losses was this testimony that the power of the Wehrmacht was definitely on the wane. Always in the past a carefully prepared and seriously launched German offensive had netted at least big early gains. This time the drive was held almost from the beginning.

For two years the Germans had fortified and strengthened Orel against this very battle. They were sure they could hold it against the best opposition the Red Army could offer. Now Orel is tottering and the Germans don't have an equally strong fortress or natural defense for at least 200 miles. Kharkov is about 300 miles due south and already threatened by a Russian salient extending west from Belgorod. Smolensk is the same distance to the northwest and likewise imperiled by the Russian line at Velikie Luki to the

(Continued on Page 2)

Sicilians Dislike Il Duce's Fascism

WITH THE AMERICAN TROOPS IN SICILY—You can't tell us that these Sicilians want to fight. Not us, not now.

Not when their kids scrounge our garbage cans for food scraps; not when their women line up along the streets laughing and cheering as our troops march through their rubbled town; not when their soldiers parade up in hundreds, hunting for somebody to surrender to.

In any one of the many towns we've captured, you can see these Sicilians walking around with civilian clothes and army boots, and you know that maybe a few days ago, these guys had guns in their hands waiting to shoot you. But maybe they saw too many of our planes dropping too many bombs, so they just dropped their guns, went home, changed clothes, and went back to work.

If it were not for the few German divisions, threatening them from the rear and for the Fascist officers who are nothing but death in an Allied victory, this show would have been over in a week. As it is, it may take a little longer. These people have nothing to fight and die for. They hate Mus-

(Continued on Page 2)

Hitler's Youth At Play

THESE TWO GERMAN YOUNGSTERS, playing at the grim game of war in the front of their home at Stuttgart, Germany, already are being molded to become model members of Hitler's Youth. This revealing photograph was found by Stars and Stripes photographer S-Sgt. Phil Stern in a portfolio belonging to Oberlieutenant Rudolph Brenner, of Stuttgart. The portfolio containing the snapshot of his children had been left behind by the Nazi officer who pulled out in a hurry when the Allies invaded Sicily.

Allies Shift Aerial Offensive To Italy

By S-Sgt. GEORGE M. HAKIM
(Stars and Stripes Staff Writer)

ALLIED FORCE HEADQUARTERS, July 23—Allied air power cast an ominous shadow over the Italian mainland this past week as American and British bombers highlighted the week's aerial activity with mass raids on the Italian capital, which was carried out by one of the largest armadas of planes ever to leave North Africa, was highly successful. The Northwest African Air Forces, coordinated with the 9th U.S. Air Force, confined all their bombs to the target area and inflicted severe damage to railroad yards, factories and an airdrome outside the city.

Heavy damage was done to the San Lorenzo marshalling yards where traffic was completely blocked. Direct hits were scored on both round houses, rolling stock and other railroad installations. The yard is an important servicing and repair center for rail facilities. Highly electrified, it is on the belt line joining with the two main lines from Florence and Naples, and on the coastal line from Genoa.

The Littorio marshalling yard, four miles to the north of Rome, was hit at least 50 times, and was 50 percent blocked to traffic. Through this important rail center passes the bulk of all freight traffic from the industrial areas of northern Italy to Rome, Naples and the southwest coast.

Both marshalling yards are of vital military importance to the Axis war strategy. They bottleneck all rail, passenger and freight traffic in the southern Italian peninsula.

Allied bombers also carried their attacks to the important Tavouelli steel plant and a large chemical works nearby. They ranged over the Ciampino airport outside the city and left several hangars and a large number of parked aircraft burning. The Littorio airport, which is near the railroad yards, was also hard-hit.

The air fighting of the past week was marked by a scarcity of

(Continued on Page 16)

Airborne Troops Held Enemy For Two Days

LONDON, July 22—The word done by U.S. airborne troops in the initial invasion of Sicily advanced Allied progress by a week, reporters were told today by Maj. Gen. Joseph M. Swing, coordinator of plans for airborne troops, who left the island a few days ago.

The airborne troops took the brunt of the attack and held off the enemy for two days until they were reinforced, Gen. Swing explained. He described their operation as the greatest airborne invasion ever attempted, larger in scope than the German attack on Crete.

Move Isolates Axis Forces In Western Part Of Sicily

By Sgt. GEORGE DORSEY
(Stars and Stripes Staff Writer)

ALLIED FORCE HEADQUARTERS, July 23—Advance elements of the American 7th Army occupied Palermo, Sicily's largest city, yesterday at 1000 hours, according to a special announcement made here today.

In view of the rapidity of its fall, Palermo could not have been seriously defended, but there were no details of the northern coastal city's capitulation in the first reports. A general statement was made here, however, which revealed that the rapidly advancing American troops met little resistance as they swept north toward their objective.

"Poorly equipped Italians showed little desire to impede the American advance," the bounprement quick bre through to the ship of an enemy convoy of Sicily was the climax of a campaign barely two weeks old.

Palermo: A City Of Lore, Lemons And Good Docks

With the fall of Palermo, the Axis has lost the largest city in Sicily and the Allies have captured their most important prize to date. Palermo has a normal population of 301,166, but during the last several months, especially since the heavy bombings began, there has been quite an exodus from Sicily and especially from such small migrations were the Paschist leader, who began to grow uneasy as time passed and sought refuge in the comparative safety of the mainland.

The port of Palermo has an important shipbuilding yard and drydock and ranks next to Genoa, Naples and Trieste as one of Italy's best ports. One of the island's finest airdromes is just outside the city. It had a reputation for throwing up more flak than any other airfield on the island.

The original city was built on a tongue of land between two inlets of the sea. The recent main street, the Cassaro Via, M'murora or Via Toledo represents the line of the ancient town with water on either side of it. The two ancient harbors

(Continued on Page 2)

Frenchmen Decorate Gen. Eisenhower

ALGIERS—Gen. Dwight D. Eisenhower, Allied Commander-in-Chief, has received France's highest decoration, the Grand Cross of the Legion of Honor, it was learned here.

Among other American and British officers who received lesser awards for their part in the Tunisian campaign was Lt. Gen. Mark W. Clark, who as Gen. Eisenhower's Deputy Commander-in-Chief helped to carry out the Allied landings in North Africa last November.

"You'll get over it, Joe. Oncet I wuz gonna write a book exposin' the army after th' war myself."

Bill Mauldin's famous infantry characters, Willie and Joe, as they appeared in his cartoon, "Up Front . . . by Mauldin," in *Stars and Stripes.*

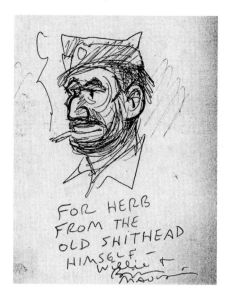

FOR HERB FROM THE OLD SHITHEAD HIMSELF— Willie + Mauld

Sketch by Bill Mauldin of his character "Willie" inscribed: "For Herb from the old shithead himself—Willie and Bill Mauldin." (Mitgang Collection)

Master Sgt. David Golding (pencil in hand), managing editor of the Mediterranean edition of *Stars and Stripes* in Rome in 1945; to his right (cigarette in hand) is Sgt. Howard Taubman, reporter and ex-*New York Times* music editor. (Golding Collection)

Tech Sgt. Irving Levinson, printing foreman of *Stars and Stripes*, closes a page in the composing room of *Il Messaggero* in Rome, 1945. (Golding Collection)

Correspondent insignia worn by Sgt. Mitgang. (Mitgang Collection)

Correspondent insignia worn by Sgt. Mitgang. (Mitgang Collection)

The infamous yellow star that the Germans forced Jews to wear in Nazi-occupied countries. This French one says *Juif* (Jew). The author obtained it in a refugee camp from a liberated Frenchwoman. (Mitgang Collection)

An armband, imprinted with the American flag, worn by the author when he was in the Air Corps, during the invasion of Casablanca in 1942; also worn when, as a correspondent, he accompanied the British parachutists landing in Greece in 1944. (Mitgang Collection)

General Eisenhower at SHAPE headquarters in France, in February 1952. Photo is inscribed: "For Herbert Mitgang—with best wishes to a veteran of the Mediterranean campaign in World War II." Ike befriended and defended *Stars and Stripes.* (Mitgang Collection)

Herbert Mitgang with General Eisenhower on the Normandy beachhead during filming of a TV documentary, *D-Day Plus Twenty Years,* in summer 1963. The film was written by the author. (Mitgang Collection)

Herbert Mitgang at his typewriter (before computers) in the *New York Times* when he was an editorial writer and member of the editorial board in the 1960s and 1970s. (*Times* studio photo)

Herbert Mitgang and David Golding, who was managing editor of *Stars and Stripes* in Rome. This photograph was taken at a nostalgic reunion in New York in 1990. (Mitgang Collection)

CHAPTER 7

Palermo II

The Contessa's Wedding Cake

*T*HE STARS AND STRIPES staff slept and ate in the Albergo Elena, a clean, second-class hotel on Piazza Giulio Cesare. I loved the fact that the street next to the hotel was named Via Lincoln, in honor of the sixteenth American President during our Civil War, at a time when Garibaldi and his Redshirts were liberating the island and helping to unify Italy.

Across a narrow alleyway, our balcony faced the balcony of a modern apartment building. Sgt. Bill Hogan and I were standing on our balcony, puffing on our Chesterfields and studying the action in the busy street below—*ragazzi* kicking a soccer ball, an organ grinder cranking out Puccini arias, hawkers peddling candied almonds in paper cones—when an elegant, well-coiffed woman who looked to be about forty years old waved at us from her facing balcony, and motioned with her fingers to her lips that she also wanted a smoke.

We smiled in recognition of her message, and she lowered a straw basket to the ground. Following her directions, a ragazzo picked up the basket and carried it across the alleyway to our albergo and balcony. As a messenger fee, we gave the kid his asking price—two cigarettes, "one for now and one for later"—and placed a half-pack and a matchbook in the basket for the woman.

The kid referred to her as "the Contessa."

She lowered a rope to retrieve the basket and yanked it up carefully.

When the basket was on her balcony, she shouted to us, in English, "Thank you, kind gentlemen."

We returned the compliment in our language-lesson Italian, with a cheerful "Grazie."

A few moments later, she lit up, inhaled deeply, and waved her cigarette at us.

We were delighted by her obvious pleasure.

The next day, a hand-written letter was delivered to Signor Herbert Mitgang, managing editor—somehow she had learned my name and position, probably by reading a copy of *Stars and Stripes*—on engraved stationery with a coat-of-arms, from Contessa Elisabetta Ustica. It was an invitation to me and for two of "my balcony friends" to join her for afternoon tea on the following Saturday at precisely 4 P.M.

On the appointed day, I asked Bill Estoff and Bill Hogan to join me so they could share in the memory of having tea with a genuine Sicilian countess in the midst of war. It was something to write home about. War was hell, indeed.

We put on freshly pressed shirts without any ink stains. The Contessa was dressed in a long-sleeved Fortuny dress and wore a hat with a veil. She greeted us as if we were fellow members of a royal family, then tinkled a handbell once. Her maid responded by bringing out a silver tea service. The Contessa herself graciously poured our tea.

We offered her a cigarette and insisted that she take another one "for later."

She modestly asked us to call her Elisabetta rather than "Contessa," and we, in turn, told her our first names and where we lived in the States—Estoff in Syracuse, Hogan in San Francisco, and me in Brooklyn. She asked me if Brooklyn was near New York, and I told her it was a borough within New York City.

How did she speak English so well?

"As a child, I was sent to boarding school in London."

I told her that I was doubly pleased to be addressed as "Mr." on her letterhead because it reminded me that I was a civilian under arms and only a soldier "for the duration of the war."

The Contessa said, "I enjoy reading your Army newspaper, but I don't understand the jokes and I cannot find the slang words in my dictionary. What is a GI?"

We told her it stood for Government Issue—an ordinary soldier.

"But you gentlemen are not ordinary," she said cordially. "You are journalists."

Then, half in English and half in Italian, the Contessa got down to business: "Are any of you married or do you have a fiancée at home waiting for you?"

Bill Estoff and Bill Hogan obviously didn't understand her question—neither one of them was married nor engaged. Nevertheless, to appear polite they both nodded.

I replied that I was single and not engaged to anyone.

Whereupon, the Contessa summoned her maid again and asked her to show Estoff and Hogan to the door, saying rather imperiously that she did not wish to take them away from their journalistic duties any longer—"Perhaps another time, gentlemen. Goodbye."

So ended the tea party for them.

When I also got up to leave, the Contessa commanded, "Mr. Herbert, you stay right here."

Once again, she tinkled her bell three times—signaling it somewhat differently. At the same time, the Contessa called out, "Dorotea!"

From another room entered a smiling young lady of about eighteen or nineteen.

"Mr. Herbert, may I introduce my dear niece, Dorotea. And, Dorotea, this gentleman is Mr. Herbert, a famous American journalist from Brooklyn, New York City."

"Enchanted," said Dorotea, extending her hand a bit nervously.

"Tell him your name in English," the Contessa ordered.

"Dorothy," Dorotea instantly answered.

"She is a senior at the University of Palermo, and hopes to continue her graduate studies in the United States, under the right circumstances and with proper residency," the Contessa said. "I think that is a wonderful idea, don't you, Mr. Herbert?"

"Yes, of course," I politely replied. "A student from Palermo would surely be welcome."

Now the Contessa herself went into the kitchen and emerged bearing a large round cake with some decorated words on it that I couldn't make out.

She broke the cake in two, gave half to Dorotea, who didn't leave a crumb, and handed me the other half.

Suddenly, a light bulb went on in my head!

I declined my half, patting my stomach, as if to indicate that I was too full or too fat to eat.

Then I stood up and headed for the door.

Contessa Elisabetta squeezed my arm.

Before I left, she whispered in my ear, "I guarantee you that Dorotea is a virgin."

I blushed.

We shook hands, I thanked her for the hospitality, and hurriedly made my exit.

Back at the Albergo Elena, Bill Estoff and Bill Hogan were waiting for me.

"Mit, what happened?" Estoff asked me. "Your face is all red—you look a little sick."

"I almost got engaged to marry the Contessa's niece," I explained. "The Contessa rolled out a fancy Sicilian cake, broke it in half, her niece ate half, and I was offered the second half. Finally, I woke up! I knew if I ate my half I'd be hooked—so I ran the hell out as fast as I could!"

"You jerk," Estoff said. "Didn't you realize something was wrong when Hogan and I were practically kicked out of her house?"

Bill Hogan broke in. "Maybe you ought to think about it. The niece is probably royal, too. Maybe you could become a duke or something if you married her. Arise, Sir Herbert, Duke of Brookalino!"

"Sorry, I'm only a commoner. I'll pass my dukedom to you, friend. Sir William, Duke of the Golden Gate and San Francisco—that sounds much better."

"You're both nuts," said Bill Estoff, the ex-bookie whose name I had put on the masthead as sports editor. Actually, he handled our circulation. "The whole deal looks like a fixed horse race to me. From now on, no more butts for the Contessa."

We still waved to the Contessa and I continued to fill her lowered basket with loose Lucky Strikes (not my brand). But no more invitations came for afternoon tea from Contessa Elisabetta Ustica. She retained her dignity and we our innocence.

And so, Mr. Herbert missed his chance to produce half-royal bambini and remained a commoner.

On Christmas Day, 1943, Lt. Burchard and I invited all the ragazzi who hung around the Albergo Elena restaurant with tin cans hoping for our leftover food to a sit-down Christmas dinner.

We ordered our slow-witted mess corporal, who did double duty as a circulation driver, to requisition ten extra turkey dinners.

He refused to do so, saying, "It's against Army regulations to requisition GI chow for civilians—I could get into a lot of trouble with 7th Army headquarters."

Sgt. Stanley Meltzoff, who overheard us, shook his clenched fist and threatened to punch the mess corporal in the nose unless the extra dinners were delivered.

Jim and I patted Meltzoff approvingly on the shoulder; the mess corporal got the message and returned an hour later with the extra dinners.

After the *Stars and Stripes* staff ate, the young boys arrived, scrubbed and dressed in their Sunday best. Without their tattered street clothes, we hardly recognized them.

We dismissed Lena and Lola, the two waitresses, gave them some holiday rations, and told them to go home to their families— we would serve the ragazzi.

Then the next obstacle arose. Luigi, the proprietor of the hotel and restaurant, refused to allow the boys to sit at the tables where we usually ate. He called them a gang of little street thieves who would steal his silverware.

We promised Luigi that nothing would be stolen.

Once again, Jim pulled his convincing .45 from its holster.

Luigi fell to his knees and begged for his life. He said he would serve the boys "subito pronto."

After the dinners were warmed in the kitchen, Estoff, Hogan, and I replaced Lena and Lola as the waiters while Luigi glowered and counted the silverware.

He muttered to his wife in the kitchen that "three crazy American sergeants" were serving the ragazzi.

The boys gobbled down the turkey, cranberry sauce, and sweet potatoes, but only ate half of their portions. We wondered if they didn't like the American Army's traditional holiday food. But that wasn't the reason. All of them had brought along tin cans and filled them with their own leftovers to take home to their brothers and sisters.

That Christmas of 1943 when we fed and served our half-starved Sicilian youngsters was the merriest Christmas of my life in or out of uniform. I truly believe our kindness created unforgettable goodwill for the United States.

★ CHAPTER 8 ★

Greece

With the British Parachutists

W HILE REPORTING from Advanced Allied Force headquarters in Rome—after closing down the Sicily edition—I got wind of the fact that British parachutists were planning to retake German-occupied Greece. I put in a request to the Brits that I would like to accompany them on their mission.

I was told, in no uncertain terms, that not only could I not join the parachutists, but I would not be allowed anywhere near their operation.

"This is strictly a British show," said the British public information officer, a lieutenant colonel. And, he added, pulling rank, "You Yanks won't be allowed to write about our operation—repeat, OUR operation. We have our own reporters from the United Kingdom who are going to cover our own men, without any of our esteemed American allies trying to take credit away from our lads."

After that putdown, there was no appeal to higher authority at Allied Force Headquarters. But the notion that an American journalist—especially someone in uniform—would not report the story fairly was too much to swallow.

I decided to get some background information for my paper because there would have to be a story in *Stars and Stripes* on such a big deal as the return to Greece. So I went down to the airfield in Southern Italy where the British parachutists were preparing for their bold adventure.

What luck! I discovered that the parachutists were being carried to the drop zone by the American 51st Wing. That would be my excuse for reporting the British operation.

I would cover our American troop carriers—no one could stop me from doing that. I correctly suspected that in the turmoil of such an operation I'd be able to report the full story of what I had seen.

First, I filed a short piece about the seasoned American 51st Wing, reporting that their planes had been in the invasions of Sicily and southern France. These unarmed C-47s had also dropped thousands of pounds of supplies to the anti-Nazi partisans in the Balkans.

I was happy to be able to get a favorable quote from one of the 51st's pilots complimenting the British: "This parachute unit has the toughest guys in the business. The American paratroopers sweat it out a little more and are cockier. But paratroopers are paratroopers—they've all got guts."

I got another lucky break. While in southern Italy, I ran into one of the fliers from my old Air Corps outfit, the 5th Wing. He told me that Tex McCrary, a *New York Daily News* writer who was now serving as an Air Corps P.R. officer, was accompanying the Brits in an American medium bomber, a B-25, as an observer. After I identified myself as a *Stars and Stripes* correspondent, I was invited along for the ride to watch the British parachutists accomplish their mission with American help.

Once in the medium bomber as it flew alongside the troop carriers, I crawled forward to the unoccupied nose gunner's position so I could get a clear view of the parachutists when they hit the silk. Lying on my stomach, I began taking notes. The multicolored chutes (camouflage-green for the men, other shades for medical equipment and light weapons) opened flawlessly and fluttered to the ground.

The drop zone was outside the town of Megara—it had once been active in the Peloponnesian Wars—on the eastern end of the isthmus of Corinth. Megara was slightly to the west of Athens.

When our bomber landed on an airstrip in the drop zone, I did something that I had thought about ever since hearing about the Greek operation: I put on my armband that was imprinted with the American flag. It was the same one that I had worn during the invasion of Casablanca so that unfriendly French troops would not shoot at me. No British parachute officers objected; they wore their own Union Jack insignia.

As soon as my American flag was recognized, I was able to interview the Greek partisans who had greeted the Brits as their liberators. We discovered that the partisans had saved all our lives—they had pulled out the Krupp mines in the drop zone that the Germans had planted there, somehow knowing where the 'chutists would land. Otherwise, we all might have been blown up. I haven't been a fan of Krupp industries ever since then.

I learned that most of the partisans who cooperated with the Allies were members of the Greek Communist party; I later regretted that I was too politically innocent at the time to include this significant detail in my reporting. The partisans told me about the war crimes—including the murder of men and women in the streets who were suspected of aiding the Allies and the deportation of Jews to the concentration camps—committed by the German and Austrian SS death squads who occupied Greece.

I filed my main story (it passed censorship without any problems—except that for security reasons I wasn't allowed to mention what the different color chutes held) for the Mediterranean edition of *Stars and Stripes* in Rome the next day.

BRITISH STRIKE FINAL MEDITERRANEAN BLOW

By Sgt. Herbert Mitgang

IN A B-25 OVER GREECE, Oct. 14, [1944]—The last airborne-seaborne attack against the Mediterranean end of Europe was pulled off by a unit of British parachutists at high noon today in the first phase of a combined Allied operation directed against the retreating German forces in Greece.

Hot Lips, our American medium bomber hot-piloted by Lt. Charlie Barnett, of Los Angeles, wove into the formation of U.S. C-47s, which rallied from several airfields in Southern Italy, at a point over the Ionian Sea. In the giant aerial armada, British parachutists anxiously and cooly awaited for the moment when they would reach their destination.

That moment came shortly after noon over Megara airfield that was dotted with wrecked Swastika-marked Luftwaffe aircraft in the wildest country imaginable. A strong wind whipped across the Gulf of Corinth and for several minutes before the 'chutists hit the silk it looked as if they would be blown into the water. But there was no need for a single one of the maroon-beretted Britons to use his Mae West, although every man was prepared for a little dunking.

As planned, the pilots gave the green light at the precise coordinated moment. Down went the human cargo, first laterally to their aircraft and then straight down to the earth, where three years before they had been kicked out by paratroopers from Germany.

As the tough Britons soared to the ground borne by their silk chutes, men, women, and children applauded and helped them out of their rigging.

The units, including English, Scottish, and Welsh battalions, were guided to the drop zone by a small force from SBS (Special Boat Service), who are parachutists commanded by Lt. Col. George Jellicoe, an English earl, who is the only son of Admiral Jellicoe, hero of the Battle of Jutland in World War I. Each parachutist carried, in addition to his battle gear, two weeks advance pay. And one of the men carried his income tax blank—"and I hope it gets lost," he told me.

No opposition was encountered at the airfield. The enemy had picked up his booty, committed his atrocities, and departed two days before. This was the rule all along the southern boundaries of Greece. Jellicoe's men entered Megara without a scrap, though land mines were encountered. I noticed the empty containers labeled Krupp on the ground; at that moment, I hoped that the Krupp owners would be remembered and tried as war criminals after the war.

The chutes were picked up by Greek civilians, but one excited partisan with a couple of bandoleers made everyone turn in his chute and gear to the Britons, who seemed disinterested in claiming them.

One British parachutist, however, seeing one of his men cutting up a chute, said: "You'll never win this bloody war by cutting them up. Each one costs 94 bloody pounds." The soldier explained that he wanted to use it to cover up his Bren gun rather than to make a distinctive scarf.

Some of the precious silk and rayon was carried away to a nearby town—to make a wedding gown for a bride as a gift from the United Nations.

A half hour after landing, the sky soldiers were lined up and ready to move after the fleeing enemy beyond Athens. It was not known whether the Germans had destroyed the Marathon Dam, which supplies Athenians with water.

Other chutes which continued to drop all afternoon carried supplies for the British warriors. The 51st Wing, commanded by Col. Timothy Manning of Omaha, also shuttled between airfields in Italy and Greece, bearing hundreds of tons of food, medical supplies, and other necessities that the people had not seen for years.

All this time an escort of Air Corps P-38 Lightnings flew protective top cover and seemed to scribble exhaust marks in the cloudless sky.

Gliders, which had been towed in several hours before by American transport planes, carried jeeps, artillery pieces, and medical supplies. On the ground the gliders served the land purpose of headquarters and medical posts for the parachute units.

The U.S. warplanes bore their three big white bars of recognition. Some of the Greeks asked me if I knew their relatives who owned restaurants in New York City. They puzzled over the names on the C-47s: the "Ruptured Duck," the "Traveling Salesman," and "San Quentin Quail." A squadron of planes was painted with American and Chinese stars on their tails, the symbol of the Burma show.

One Welshman, who was having his sprained ankle dressed by a Greek woman doctor, compared this landing to others in the Mediterranean theater.

"This was the best one of all," he said.

As a historian, I later learned why the British public relations officer did not want me to cover the story of the British reconquest of Greece. I read a book that included the secret wartime correspondence between Roosevelt and Churchill. In rather blunt language, the two Allied leaders disagreed on the future of Greece. Churchill wanted to put the Greek king back on the throne and believed he could do so if Great Britain had greater influence there; Roosevelt favored a democratic election that would establish a republican form of government.

CHAPTER 9

Naples

Maria's Happy Place

A FTER SICILY was conquered, fierce fighting followed, led by Anglo-American forces on the Italian mainland. Hitler had ordered his generals to draw ever-new defensive lines across the Apennine Mountains after two beachhead invasions—at Salerno and Anzio—and the misguided American bombing of Montecassino Abbey, which gave the enemy a propaganda victory.

Because major attention was now devoted to the Normandy invasion, the battle for France, and the drive toward Germany in the summer and autumn of 1944, Italy became known as "the forgotten front"—except to those who fought and died there.

Strategically, the battle to conquer Italy made sense: the American 5th Army and the British 8th Army opposed and diverted a dozen German divisions from saving the Third Reich. Casualties continued to mount on both sides even as Fascist Italy, Hitler's Axis partner, collapsed. It was an old-style ground war where you actually could see your enemy. (Allied correspondents called the Germans "the Boche," "the Krauts," or simply "the

Nazis.") For the soldier-correspondents as well as the American infantrymen (affectionately nicknamed "dogfaces" or "doggies"), danger also lurked on the other side of the embattled hills.

When Naples fell, Sgt. Jack Foisie, as usual, was there with the first American foot soldiers. The intrepid *Stars and Stripes* front-line reporter scored many news beats that were the envy of civilian correspondents who did not venture as far forward. (After the war, Foisie became a renowned correspondent for the *Los Angeles Times*, covering stories all over the world.)

ONCE "BELLA NAPOLI" CAPTURED

By Sgt. Jack Foisie

Americans today patrolled the gloomy streets of once sunny Naples, a city paralyzed not so much by the Allied bombings as by systematic German sabotage of the city's municipal services— water, sanitation, light, and heat.

Destruction by German engineers began immediately following the Italian armistice and landing of Allied troops at Salerno and continued until a few hours before the advancing Allied elements, a British reconnaissance troop, and an American billeting party entered the city.

As a result Naples has become—

A city of 700,000 candles—about a candle per person.

There are no electric lights. The city hall is so dark that in wandering through the mayor's office, I mistook a mirror for a door, and perhaps my seven years of bad luck have already begun.

A city of empty looted buildings, apartment houses, and hotels. The windows were knocked out because of the bomb blasts, but the looting was done by the Germans or by incited Italians under the watchful eye of German propaganda cameras.

A city without running water; thus, without sanitation. Garbage is dumped in the nearest vacant lot for there is no transport. Flies are the thickest I've ever seen. Cats and other scavengers prowl the streets at night.

We are living at one of the few hotels that can furnish maid service and beds with clean sheets. All water, both for washing and for flushing the toilet, must be carried up seven flights of stairs.

As I look out from our bedroom balcony, I can see a mob milling at one of the few civilian water points in the city; they are like thirsty cattle at a waterhole.

This is the third day of Allied occupation of Naples and already there are indications that the chaos and despair are abating. The city is completely quiet; there is no sound of street fighting. The Luftwaffe, after a small-scale bombing and strafing of downtown Naples, has not returned. A large fighter field on the outskirts of the city has been taken over by the Allies.

Allied Military Government officials have moved in, and the usual proclamations announcing their control have been issued.

As soon as a semblance of calm descended on Naples, *Stars and Stripes* began printing a new edition at the plant of Il Mattino.

It was the first to appear on the Italian mainland. Still under the editorial command of Bob Neville, by now a lieutenant colonel, our most seasoned frontline correspondents—among them Sgts. Milton Lehman, Stanley M. Swinton, Ralph G. Martin, and Jack Foisie—reported every battle by the 5th Army. The expanded Mediterranean editions now included several experienced newspapermen—among them Howard Taubman, Jack Raymond, Hilary Lyons, and John Radosta of the *New York Times*; Ed Hill of the *New York World-Telegram*, and Lyle Dowling, a former managing editor of the *Brooklyn Eagle*.

In Master Sgt. Irving Levinson, the printing foreman who doubled as First Sergeant, we luckily had the gentlest disciplinarian in the U. S. Army—and also the most ingenious and generous.

When ink ran out, some editions of the paper actually were printed by adding a mixture of various red and white wines on the presses.

One time, Irv did a printing job for the Navy. The ship's captain rewarded him with fifty cartons of cigarettes. Irv gave everyone on the staff a carton—the wartime equivalent of passing out $50 bills.

In Naples, the *Stars and Stripes* staff was quartered in rooms on top of the Galleria Umberto Primo, in the warm heart of the city. (The encounters between the GIs and the male and female residents of Naples were described with great affection by John Horne Burns in his elegant postwar novel, *The Gallery*).

On some nights the Luftwaffe still came over to bomb the docks; to our delight, our gunners shot most of them down in flames. Shrapnel and bombs shattered all the windows in the Galleria and rain poured down through holes in the glass roof.

One of my first encounters with soldiers in Field Marshal Montgomery's British 8th Army, which was fighting the enemy on the Adriatic side of Italy, was with members of the Jewish Brigade. They carried a symbolic Star of David banner. The Jewish volunteers came from thirty-seven different countries. It took almost five years of trying before the British allowed the Jewish Brigade to be integrated into the 8th Army.

During Passover in Italy, unleavened bread (*matzoh*) and sacramental wine were sent over from Palestine to the Jewish

Brigade. In the frontlines they celebrated and sang religious prayers; enemy mortar and shellfire could not drown them out.

Members of the Jewish Brigade were introduced to me by fellow journalists who worked for the *British 8th Army News.*

"If you want to meet some real tough warriors," a British editor told me, "check out these guys in the Jewish Brigade. I've seen them in action—they're fearless and smart as hell."

A Jewish sergeant responded, "Damn right, we're smart enough not to get killed. It's the Nazis or us. The more bloody Germans we kill, the sooner the war ends and we can get down to our real business—the creation of a Jewish state of our own in Palestine."

The British editor said, "They're motivated—that's the main requirement in this man's war. It's what makes you a real soldier. I don't blame them. You know, Hitler and his henchmen are rounding up the Jews—men, women, and even children—in every country in Europe and shipping them to concentration camps. Then they're systematically gassed to death. Our intelligence has gathered the evidence from agents in some of the neutral countries who are working for us. We call these agents 'Stockholm travelers.' They slip in and out of Berlin and other German cities in the guise of businessmen. First the fucking Nazis burned books by Jewish writers and now they're burning the Jewish people. We have eyewitness accounts of what these barbarians have been doing. It's not just against the Jews—it's against Western civilization."

"Bravo!" said the Jewish Brigade sergeant.

And then a Jewish Brigade captain added something that I have never forgotten: "World War II is just a warm-up for us—we're learning tactics and how to fire the weapons for our own war of independence—just as you Yanks did when you established the United States."

Many of the Jewish Brigade veterans I encountered in Italy later served as military and political leaders in the formation of the State of Israel.

★ ★ ★

There was a refugee camp outside Naples. I spoke with dozens of Jewish men and women there who somehow had escaped from the Nazi roundups. One young woman from France still wore the compulsory yellow star on her blouse. It said "Juif" (Jew). As we talked, she ripped off the yellow star and threw it on the ground. I picked it up as evidence of what Hitler's killers were doing to identify and crucify innocent Jewish people.

Col. Bob Neville encouraged me to write the following story.

REPORT FROM A REFUGEE CAMP

By Sgt. Herbert Mitgang

A SOUTH ITALY REFUGEE CAMP—He was one of a thousand persons going to the Emergency Refugee Shelter at Fort Ontario, near Oswego, New York. Dr. Henry Hazrillak, 44, a former doctor in Belgrade, Yugoslavia, [who held the rank of major in the army, which could only resist the German invaders in those early days]. He had known their brutality himself, for a clean gauze bandage stuck out from under his shirt collar, and he had seen with his own eyes many cruel things.

And now they were going to America.

The President of the United States and the American people had consented. One thousand anti-Axis refugees from the Rome area, Southeast Italy, and Yugoslavia, hounded for years by the watchdogs of Aryanism, were traveling to freedom for the duration of the war. Then, it is contemplated, they will be returned to their homelands.

Their homes were a page from the book of dictatorial conquests: Austria, Danzig, France, Spain, Czechoslovakia, Yugoslavia, Belgium.

President Roosevelt had said: "In choosing the refugees to be brought to the United States, please bear in mind that to the extent possible those refugees should be selected for whom other havens of refuge are not immediately available. I should, however, like the group to include a reasonable proportion of various categories of persecuted people who have fled to Italy. There are real possibilities of saving human lives."

Dr. Hazrillak, like the others, was being saved. He had lived under the German jackboot in Belgrade. "A paper and pencil cannot describe what they did," he said.

"Every morning they would line up the people who would still have the spirit to defy Hitler. Jews, Communists, Nationalists, everybody was a suspect. Every day 500 people—I saw it with my own eyes—were shot by machine guns, every day for six months. After the shootings, they would string demolitions to each body and blow them up.

"And what was the crime committed by the 2,000 men and women who were put in a labor battalion for the Germans? Nobody knew. Their job was to cut wood for the Germans to keep them warm. Without food, they chopped and sawed all winter under Nazi guards. Then in January, they were found frozen stiff in the snow. Two thousand dead but that was all right—the Germans had their wood," the doctor said.

Young and old in this first group each had similar stories. Most of them did not have enough energy to express their hatred. Many walked with a padded step, toes and heels touching the ground at the same time. They had walked a long way.

The Peninsular Base Section of the U. S. Army was given the responsibility for feeding, housing, clothing, delousing, classifying, and identifying them. Medical care was provided, and that included women who were pregnant.

Ship transportation and other details of survival were jointly handled by PBS, the War Refugee Board, and a sub-commission of the Allied Control Commission. A military escort made up of selected officers and enlisted men are going with the refugees. Lt. Col. Daniel G. Talbot, of Fort Worth, Texas, is commander of this movement.

Like the other refugees, Adam Munz had many questions to ask about America. In general, he simply wanted to know if it was good, if Fort Ontario, where they were going, was like the forts and camps they had been forced to stay in before. They were all still a little dazed, confused.

Adam asked two questions: Is there much anti-Semitism in America? Will I have a chance to study?

We told him that he surely would have a chance to study, that Fort Ontario was not a concentration camp.

Sgt. Bill Estoff made sure that his trucks and mules distributed the Naples edition all the way south to our airfields around Bari and Foggia (my old outfit, the 5th Wing, flew on missions against enemy-held positions from there) and north to the battlefronts in the Apennines.

A man who enjoyed his civilian comforts, Big Bill rented a spacious apartment of his own rather than sleep in the crowded Galleria. I was delighted when he invited me to stay in one of his extra bedrooms.

Maria's place on Via Monte Dieu was in a modern apartment house where the elevator worked after you kicked it a few times. Maria was a neatly groomed woman of perhaps forty who despised the Germans because they disrupted her life, were very cheap, and spoke in a strange, guttural tongue. Her husband, an Italian Army officer, was a prisoner of war somewhere. She admired and enjoyed Americans and their largesse. Instead of paying rent in near-worthless lire, Bill Estoff supplied her with PX chocolate bars and, to be sure, tobacco—the most valuable currency. Maria was proud of her apartment and kept its rooms filled with fresh flowers for her guests. Her small staff consisted of several unmarried friends who showed up in the late morning and evening. She described them as "manicurists." They were quite independent.

I do not want to leave an impression that Maria's place was a bordello. It was simply a happy refuge from the war; it had a homelike atmosphere, with bathtubs and a shower.

One day I asked Bill Estoff if it would be all right to invite Sgt. Samuel Jones (not his real name; it's the only fictional name in this book), a *Stripes* staff correspondent who was battle-weary, to use one of the spare bedrooms for a few days. Bill was sympathetic and told Maria that there would be another guest staying overnight. A few more Baby Ruths—she was getting addicted to American candy bars—and it was a done deal.

Because of the war's deprivations, the "manicurists" sometimes were willing to add a little extra income to their own slim budgets. Maria's two regular "manicurists" were named Fedora and Mafalda.

What began as a kind deed eventually ended up as a sad tale. Samuel fell madly in love with Fedora and she with him. They came from two disparate cultures. He was a Westerner who had earned a living as a wandering cowboy. His experiences did not include familiarity with women; indeed he was rather shy in their presence. He treated Fedora with great respect; it was his first affair. Fedora was a dark-haired, top-heavy girl with peasant features. Bill Estoff described her as "well-stacked," but not in Samuel's presence.

Fedora and Sam became inseparable. She no longer would give one of her "manicures" to anyone else.

Sam told Fedora about the ranch he owned in Wyoming and that he would teach her to ride her own horse. She was thrilled at the idea. He asked Maria's permission before asking Fedora to become his fiancée.

Big Bill was pleased that, thanks to his hospitality, an old-fashioned romance had developed, and he offered to be best man at their wedding—in Napoli or Wyoming. But the path of true love hit an unexpected snag. Sam discovered that he had a case of gonorrhea. He demanded that Fedora be examined by a doctor in the Galleria who specialized in venereal diseases; the doctor confirmed that she too had contracted the same ailment. Fedora wept shamelessly. At first, Samuel apologized to Fedora for giving her gonorrhea. Ever the considerate gentleman, he obtained penicillin from an Army medical station and gave it to Fedora's physician to treat her. Both lovers denied that they had slept with anyone else. They no longer went to bed together. Without the comfort of each other's bodies, soon there were mutual recriminations.

After a few weeks, Sgt. Samuel Jones decided that it was time for him to return to reporting feature stories about GIs near the frontlines, where life was less complicated. He vaguely promised to return to Naples "soon."

Big Bill and I told Samuel that he needed a little more time and space away from Fedora before making the big decision to marry her and bring her home to the States.

So ended Samuel and Fedora's romantic interlude in Maria's happy place.

I lost track of Samuel after the war; once we exchanged Christmas cards between Brooklyn and Wyoming. No mention was made of Fedora, and I doubt she ever learned to ride a horse or cared to. Still, I wonder if, in the middle of sleepless nights, Samuel and Fedora pine for each other, recalling their idyllic wartime romance.

CHAPTER 10

Rome

"We're in Rome"

I T WAS ONE of the great coups of military or civilian journalism anywhere: as the first American troops marched into Rome in force on June 5, 1944, they were handed copies of *The Stars and Stripes* that carried the perfect banner headline. It boldly declared:

WE'RE IN ROME.

Of course, the Page 1 five-column headline had a double meaning: The soldiers had captured the Italian capital on June 4 and within twenty-four hours their own newspaper was there to greet them and describe their feat.

In the vanguard of the infantrymen who conquered the center of Mussolini's Fascist government was an advance crew of *Stars and Stripes* editorial personnel. They made a dash for the plant of *Il Messaggero*, the independent newspaper at No. 152, Via del Tritone. Among those whose names appeared on the masthead of the early editions of the paper were Sgts. Milton

Lehman, Albert Kohn, Paul Green, George Dorsey and Jack Raymond. (Al Kohn was later killed in southern France.)

The lead story in Vol. 1, No. 1 of the new edition, by Sgt. Paul Green, reported that after liberating Rome, Allied forces pursued the Germans fleeing northward. And to give the readers historical perspective, an article by Herbert L. Matthews, the chief *New York Times* correspondent, was printed. It noted that Allied generals had succeeded where Hannibal had failed centuries before.

The erudite Matthews wrote:

"Rome has been reached, goal of conquerors throughout the ages, none of whom has ever been able to make the almost impossible south-to-north campaign. What Hannibal didn't dare, Generals Alexander, Clark, Montgomery, and Leese accomplished, but at such a cost in blood and matériel and time that it will probably never be again attempted in history."

Soon *Stars and Stripes* began its own buildup in Rome. Veteran reporters, editors, and printers arrived from North Africa, Sicily, and Naples to turn out the most complete and professional military newspaper ever produced. It was called the Mediterranean edition. Col. Neville was still in command as the publications officer. Master Sgt. David Golding was managing editor, Sgt. William Hogan was news editor, and I was head of the copydesk. Under the editorship of Sgt. John M. Willig, a Sunday magazine section was added, covering frontline, stateside, and worldwide news. Thanks to Col. Neville's broad knowledge of foreign affairs, the magazine included information about the future role of the United Nations.

Together with longtime companions from earlier *Stars and Stripes* editions, it was my good fortune to live and work in Rome during the Italian campaign. To walk through the streets was to walk through history—viewing monuments, churches, and buildings from different eras; only the overwhelming granite Victor Emmanuel Monument and Mussolini's ugly official Fascist structures seemed out of character in the ancient city.

Every morning, I walked slowly from our requisitioned hotel, Albergo Nazionale, which had a roof garden, taking in my surroundings. There was a Berlitz language school on the ground floor of the hotel, where young Italian students replied to my polite "Buon giorno!" with their jolly new English, "Good morning!"

To reach our offices at *Il Messaggero* from the hotel, I usually took a rambling walk that passed the Trevi Fountain, where I paused to watch the old caretaker adjust the flow of the water and fish for coins. Along Via del Tritone, I observed Roman office workers rushing to their desks, noticing the men carrying Florentine leather briefcases of authority, the women balancing themselves on cork heels and soles, and the long-skirted priests heading for one of the numerous seminaries and churches.

After the despised German presence in the city, the Romans regarded Americans as liberators. It was pleasant to get a V-for-victory greeting from strangers. They knew about us from old Hollywood films that played again and again in their movie houses during the war. Sometimes civilians asked me if I knew "Fred and Ginger"—their favorite dancers—and if they were going to make any new pictures. I reassured them that Fred Astaire and Ginger Rogers would go on forever.

The American and Allied soldiers on leave enjoyed Italian food and discovered the friendly restaurants in Trastevere; one or two served kosher meals. Outdoor dining was a new and pleasant experience. The Romans directed us to the sights, especially the museums. A small crowd would happily assemble to give us directions if we looked lost.

One of my most memorable evenings was spent at the Rome Opera House, where I saw a fine performance of Puccini's *Tosca*. The dramatic third act takes place, of course, on a parapet of the Castel Sant'Angelo in Rome.

After the opera, I crossed the Tiber and walked home along the river. Looking up, I saw the actual Castel Sant'Angelo—just as I had seen it reproduced so faithfully on stage in the final act of the opera only moments before. It gave me a feeling of deja vu that could only have happened in *bella Roma*. I envision that scene whenever I listen to a recording of *Tosca* or see it performed at the Metropolitan Opera House in Lincoln Center.

★ ★ ★

One of the personalities on the *Stars and Stripes* staff who made life cheerful for everyone was Sgt. George McCoy, who worked alongside Bill Estoff in the circulation department. In civilian life, McCoy had been an actor and broadcaster, conducting a nightly radio interview show in New York. It always began: "This is George (the Real) McCoy, speaking to you from the steps of the Astor Hotel in New York. Is there anybody here from out of town?"

In his spare time, he continued almost the same opening pitch in Rome for the Armed Forces Radio Network: "This is Sgt. George (the Real) McCoy, speaking to you from below Mussolini's old balcony in the Piazza Venezia in Rome. Is there anybody here from out of town?"

Of course, every GI that he interviewed was from "out of town." They loved to be heard on his show. Sgt. McCoy had a repertoire of a hundred wisecracks. His humor took full advantage of the fact that he was speaking in the Piazza Venezia where the silenced Fascist dictator no longer wowed the crowds. George

McCoy's radio program symbolized another victory for the Yanks in Italy.

One of the great additions to the *Stars and Stripes* staff in Rome was Cpl. Klaus Mann, novelist (*Mephisto*) and playwright, who was the son of Thomas Mann, the Nobel laureate in literature, then living in California. His literary articles ran in our magazine section. Once in a while, I edited one of his astute pieces. To no avail, I would plead with Klaus to write shorter paragraphs or break his book-length paragraphs in half, explaining that he was writing for narrow newspaper columns.

Having been a victim of Hitlerism, Klaus brought a personal view to his writings and underscored what the war was all about for everybody—his colleagues as well as our readers.

MY OLD COUNTRYMEN

By Cpl. Klaus Mann

First came the greetings from the president, then came the physical examination. When I was through with the physical, and was found all right, the psychiatrist had a word with me. He was a busy man, the psychiatrist at the Grand Central Palace, New York. Rather in a hurry, he seemed to be. He asked me only one question.

"You're of German origin, aren't you—well, then, do you really feel capable of fighting Germans?"

I said, "Yes, Sir, I do!"

And I am afraid that I grinned a little while saying it. The question struck me as funny.

But in the course of my life in the Army, I was asked the same question repeatedly: "How do men like yourself, of

German birth and, until recently, of German citizenship, feel fighting against former countrymen?"

Maybe the question isn't so very funny, after all. It is not quite easy, perhaps, for any non-German person to understand why those most familiar with Germany are most eager and determined to fight Nazism and to help wipe out that obnoxious plague. I am sure that I speak also for the thousands of other former German citizens now active in the various armies of the United Nations in saying our militant resolution has a two-fold psychological and moral source: first, our natural loyalty to a new homeland to which we are deeply indebted; and, second, our intimate first-hand knowledge of the mortal danger which Hitlerism means to civilization.

To me, as to most of the other German fugitives from Nazi terrorism, it was a matter of course to contribute our humble bit to the war effort of the democracies. In fact, I hardly felt that I was changing my status or the essential purpose of my life when I became an American soldier. Rather, it seemed to me that my new job was to continue doing with new weapons and under new conditions what I had been doing all along for the past ten years. To fight Hitler, and everything Nazism stands for, was indeed my main occupation, ever since the Nazi dictatorship was established in 1933.

My family and I left the Reich voluntarily, as did many other Germans, as soon as Hitler came to power. We left although—not being Jews and not being affiliated with any political party—we might have been acceptable to the ruling gang. We left because we felt that a country taken over by the Nazis would be an impossible place to live in—a place where the very air was stifling and poisonous. We left because we realized that Hitler would inevitably lead the German nation to war, to disgrace, and to disaster.

We might have thought and acted differently—in fact, we might have found that it would be more useful and more honorable to stay at home if there had been a chance to fight Nazism within Germany. But there was no such chance—especially in the case of people who were so notorious, from the Nazi point of view, as the Mann tribe. There was my father, who had given quite a bit of trouble to the German nationalists, even before 1933; my uncle, Heinrich Mann—a veteran champion of German liberalism and anti-fascism; my sister Erika, who is a war correspondent, and my scholarly but tough younger brother, Golo—also a member of the American army. Too numerous and too conspicuous to go underground, we had to choose between compromise and exile. We had to make up our own minds—either to play ball with the Nazis or to give up our country. We preferred the latter.

By doing so, we did not betray what had been fine and lovable in pre-Hitler Germany; on the contrary, we made a desperate effort to save it.

The German anti-Nazis in exile—that is, those among them who were politically conscious and active—had the double mission of warning both the world and their former countrymen against Nazism. We kept imploring the Germans: Get rid of Hitler! He is your undoing; he will ruin you! But the Germans were deaf. Most of them believed in Hitler as the Messiah—sent by God to increase the greatness and glory of the Fatherland.

So we cried out to the world: Beware of Hitler and of the German people who follow him! Hitler means war. Get rid of him, lest you have war on a worldwide scale. But the world was not able, or not willing to accept or even to consider any advice or warning from those who had no illusions about the dead seriousness of the Hitler challenge. The world wanted peace at any price—even at the price of appeasing the archenemy of peace, Adolf Hitler.

The archenemy, meanwhile, became stronger and stronger. In the end he was so powerful that he could no longer be appeased. The great showdown became inevitable.

Could people of our kind stay aloof under such circumstances? Could we waver? Could we hesitate?

We had failed twice in our historical duty. We had not succeeded in preventing Nazism in Germany, and our voices had been too weak to arouse public opinion to the imminence of the Nazi danger. Now we had the opportunity to make good, to a certain extent, our previous failures. Now we had the chance to prove the sincerity of our convictions by participating in the fight against Nazi barbarism.

The complete defeat and extinction of the Hitler regime is a vital necessity, not only for my new homeland, the United States of America, but also for the whole world. If we Americans of German stock cherish freedom and peace, we have to help in defending those supreme values—even if the aggressors happen to be our former countrymen.

All of us on *Stripes* who became friends with the Italian people heard tales of atrocities committed by the Germans and their Fascist stooges against anyone suspected of aiding the Allies by rescuing downed fliers or helping American prisoners to escape or hiding Jews who were being rounded up for shipment to the Nazi concentration camps.

Some of the experiences of the Jews—many of whom served as partisans in the resistance movement, risking their necks to sabotage the German forces behind the lines and rescue downed Allied airmen—were described in *Stars and Stripes* by our correspondents, such as this report from the post-liberation Roman ghetto.

By Sgt. Jack Raymond

If you walk through the narrow, cobbled streets of the so-called Jewish ghetto in Rome, behind the great synagogue on the Tiber, you will be greeted on every hand by the storekeepers, the shop workers, the housewives, and their children who will salute you with a pleasant 'Shalom' ('Peace') say these people who have known little peace.

They will invite you to sit and chat with them awhile and soon you will realize that in their hearts there is a great thankfulness toward the Christians who sheltered them against the Nazi-pursued Fascists. Deeds both simple and heroic have been indelibly recorded in the legends of the community and their heroes range from poor and simple neighbors who knew well the lessons of human brotherhood to strong voices in church and state whose benevolence was not in the slightest weakened by personal unconcern.

Listen to these people and you will learn that after the Nazis came last September and the Jews fled about the Eternal City like deer in the forest who hear the sound of the hunter, these things came to pass:

In an institution devoted to Catholic worship, Jews gathered to conduct their Holy Sabbath services.

In a Catholic orphanage, where youngsters pondered over the lessons of the catechisms, children of Israel shared their simple rations of food and clothing.

In a convent, nuns who had carefully noted the calendar prepared a surprise Passover feast that included rice instead of leavened bread for a group of Jewish women.

As they relate these stories, the Jews of Rome remember well the incident of the 50 kilos of gold. On last September 26, the Nazis called upon the leaders of the Jewish community to supply within 24 hours 50 kilos of gold on threat of taking heads of families as hostages. That money was supplied, but the Jews will tell you that if it hadn't been for the unsolicited contributions of Catholic neighbors it could not have been done. Non-Fascist Italian officials obtained gold from the black market to aid the cause. It is known, too, that from the Vatican itself there came an offer of 15 kilos, but by that time the ransom had been collected.

There is an apocryphal story that on the day of the Allied liberation of Rome, prayers for the Pope were offered in the Jewish synagogue on Longo Tevere, and that cheers went up in his honor. Dr. Israel Zolli, chief rabbi of Rome, explains that this is not so, that it was a passerby's exclamation of gratitude which gave rise to the story. But, he adds, if we did not hold special services for the Pope, if we did not then raise loud our voices in praise of the people who had helped us, it must only be that the Catholic church and Christians in general had given us a demonstration of goodness of heart and kindness for which we had not words enough to express adequate gratitude.

On the night of July 24, Rabbi Zolli conducted prayer services in thanks for the aid rendered the Jews by the church authorities of the Vatican, and those services were broadcast and radioed throughout the world.

Pope Pius's silence while Jews were persecuted, arrested, and shipped north on the death trains to concentration camps has been criticized by people of different faiths, including Catholics. The wartime pope even failed to speak out when Hitler's racial laws were enacted by Mussolini's Fascist regime. Church historians have since written that had the pope objected to the anti-Semitic actions, Catholics in Germany and elsewhere might have heeded him and not participated in the persecution of the innocent Jewish people. Succeeding popes have deplored the wartime silence by the Vatican and spoken out against anti-Semitism.

It is noteworthy that on their own, sometimes individual priests and nuns bravely hid men, women, and children during roundups by the Nazis in Italy. I met some of these priests in Tuscany.

The Italian campaign crossed the Adriatic Sea in pursuit of the enemy in Yugoslavia and Greece. Sometimes special British and American soldiers fought alongside partisans who were sympathetic to the Allied cause. A small group of Americans described their experiences to Sgt. Stanley Swinton, one of our frontline reporters. (After the war, Stan became a foreign correspondent for the Associated Press—he served as chief of the Rome bureau and then was promoted to be vice president and director of the AP's World News Service.)

In this piece for *Stripes*, Stan deliberately disguised the location of his interviews by using a blind dateline—for security reasons—because these daring warriors operated in secrecy and were hunted by the Germans and collaborators.

By Sgt. Stanley M. Swinton

SOMEWHERE IN ITALY—The strange band of bearded men munched upon cheese and corn bread in their hill hideout. Conversation came in broken pieces, a jargon of Greek and accented English. Finally, the lieutenant spat an olive pit and gave orders to move out.

Slowly the men worked their way across the wild terrain toward the Salonika-Athens railroad. Moonlight silhouetted protruding weapon shapes: BARs, tommy guns, bazookas, and grenades. Close to their objective, flank patrols broke off toward the right and left. The core of men slipped noiselessly forward to the rail line. Between two German machine guns spaced fifty yards to each side, they went to work, planting explosives. They were back in the craggy hills again before an echoing explosion thundered the end of a Nazi evacuation train.

Next day the German radio shrieked that "battalions of Yankee terrorists" were operating against them. An announcer warned of "regiments of American cavalry." At their secret rendezvous, the American GIs listened and laughed. Never, from the hour on May 11, when the first eleven U.S. soldiers parachuted down, until our guerrilla forces were withdrawn late in November, were there more than 250 American combat men in Greece. Operating in small, compact bands, they stabbed almost nightly at German highway and rail communications. Along with Greek guerrillas and British soldiers, the American mountain fighters helped to shatter enemy evacuation plans.

Today the American GIs who fought in Greece, as well as their comrades in Yugoslavia, have returned to Italy. Shorn of their heavy beards and their uniforms stripped of souvenirs, they resemble any other Americans.

To give the Mediterranean edition an American feeling, Master Sgt. Irv Levinson arranged for color comic strips for the Sunday paper; this section had to be inserted by hand—to the amusement of the Italian printers in the pressroom at *Il Messaggero*. To be sure, some of us felt that running comic strips alongside serious war reporting was frivolous. But if the "jokes" made our GI readers feel they were reading their hometown papers in the States, well, that was the idea.

Once in a great while, Lt. Col. Bob Neville, our worldly and experienced commanding officer, would contribute a historical essay to remind our youthful *Stars and Stripes* readers about the origins, atrocities, and aims of the Second World War. In a reminiscing byline piece (omitting his rank), he described what it was like to be in Warsaw just before the Nazis invaded Poland. Then, in the final days of combat in Italy, Bob wrote this article about the war and also reminded us of President Roosevelt's vision for the future.

By Robert Neville

By the time of the fall of Warsaw, the die had long been cast. Hitler had been advertising for months that Poland was his next objective. It seems curious now to reflect that a lot of people doubted the Fuehrer's words.

The rise and decline of the Hitler empire can be charted by certain activities. The Reichstag fire, February 1933, a Nazi plot, was used by Hitler as the excuse to liquidate all democratic liberties. Books were burned. Repression of Jews, churches, trade unions, began. Concentration camps were started. Germany left the League of Nations. In January 1939, Hitler had divided and conquered without war. Austria was annexed. Appeasement was temporarily triumphant at Munich, and Czechoslovakia was offered up as the victim. Denmark, Norway, and France were overrun. Only the British held on and then withstood the might of the Luftwaffe. . . .

The inauguration of Franklin D. Roosevelt for his fourth term and Harry S. Truman for his first term as vice president, was a simple ceremony that cost the nation only $2,000.

President Roosevelt said: "We Americans, together with the Allies, are passing through a period of supreme test. It is a test of our courage—our resolve—our wisdom—our essential decency—and if we meet that test honorably—we shall perform a service of historic importance which men, women and children will honor for all time."

(Rereading Roosevelt's words, I am reminded of the fact that I was old enough to have voted for him on a soldier's ballot overseas for his fourth term as president.)

Toward the end of 1944, Lt. Col. Neville asked me to go back to North Africa and consolidate the Casablanca and Oran editions because the war had moved onward to Europe. He said that I could take along one of our young correspondents. I invited Sgt. Peter Furst, a bright reporter and talented artist, to accompany me. (Like Klaus Mann, Peter had been a refugee from Germany who had settled in the States. After the war, he became a distinguished professor of anthropology.) I was pleased when Peter agreed to join me.

In Oran, I found the usual chaos at the paper. Too many girlfriends were hanging out there with the printers. Compared to Algiers, the city itself was still ugly and unexciting. I had not yet read the French Existentialists, particularly Albert Camus, author of *La Peste* (*The Plague*), which is set in Oran.

But I found some comfort in speaking to French newspapermen at a nearby bar called the "Cafe Ou Tout Va Bien" (Cafe Where All Goes Well). One of them asked me, "Why is *Stars and Stripes* printing at *L'Echo d'Oran*—giving them your business and prestige—instead of at *Le Republicain*? *L'Echo* was pro-Vichy and anti-de Gaulle." I did not know the answer, except to say that we Americans were not familiar with French politics early in the war—and perhaps afterward, too.

It took only a few weeks in North Africa to combine the two *Stripes* editions. Then, Peter Furst and I cheerfully returned to bella Roma and civilization, rejoining our companions on the Mediterranean edition of *The Stars and Stripes*.

CHAPTER 11

Florence and Pisa

Combat in Tuscany

WANTED TO SEE the Renaissance cities of Tuscany before the Nazis destroyed them and looted all the art treasures for the Third Reich's museums and the private collections of Adolf Hitler and Hermann Goering. The River Arno running through Florence and Pisa formed part of the defensive line for the German forces; the enemy held the northern side of these cities.

After a little pleading that it was my turn to cover "the front," I wrapped up my desk duties in Rome and pointed a jeep in the direction of 5th Army Forward headquarters in a wooded area somewhere south of the Arno, between Pisa and Florence.

Before I left, Bob Neville and Dave Golding cautioned me: "Your only job is to send back lots of human interest pieces, not to get yourself killed. Don't take any dumb chances—we don't need any heroes."

My windshield was down and covered with tarpaulin—any fool knew that glass reflected and could draw artillery fire or even a Luftwaffe fighter seeking a target of opportunity.

I was driving along happily and humming to myself because everything I needed was with me in my jeep: my old Air Corps Springfield rifle and a couple of ammo clips, a scrounged .25-calibre Italian Beretta that I wore as a sidearm, two five-gallon cans of gasoline, one steel helmet (I wore the liner as a sun shade) that rattled around in the back, several days' worth of C and K rations, five gallons of water, two canteens (one held vino) and—most irreplaceable of all—one portable typewriter.

That little noiseless Remington was a mark of my military trade as an Army correspondent. I could set it down anywhere— on an empty ammunition box or in a foxhole. Unlike the civilian correspondents, I was armed; I didn't have to be, but in unfamiliar places I felt it was important for my weapons to be visible even if I didn't expect to fire them.

As I drove along the Ligurian Sea coastal road, checking my map and identifying the island of Elba on my left but not thinking about Napoleon's or anyone else's war, I passed by the hill towns of Tuscany. Looking up at the towers of San Gimignano, at that moment I imagined knights in armor mounted on steeds charging down the mountain slopes. Now there were all-too-real 20th-century enemies: German Huns.

There were non-combat service units everywhere—what we jokingly called "mess kit repair battalions"—that were hard to resist writing about. They were okay for short pieces—for the "flashes from the front" column.

I pressed on to get to the combat outfits.

After getting a cot and a tent assignment at 5th Army Forward headquarters, near a village (whose name didn't appear on my military map), I got a briefing in the Operations tent.

At a bar in the village, I vividly recall having a long evening's talk with a priest from Arezzo. I took notes for a piece about how he had helped the anti-Fascist *partigani* (the partisans) and the Yanks.

The priest told me about the art of the carillonneur. He described how his bell ringing not only summoned people to church but also regulated their births, weddings, and deaths.

HUMBLE AREZZO FRIAR UNLIKE USUAL HEROES

By Sgt. Herbert Mitgang

The humble friar from the Chiesa San Domenico in Arezzo who twice faced a Nazi firing squad is too self-effacing to tell all the details. History demands that its heroes be colorful, but Fra Raimondo, a Dominican father, avoids colorful language. He calls himself "ordinary."

To Allied artillerymen and to a few thousand people in Arezzo, the friar is extraordinary. When the Germans occupied his city, he became the mayor because the Fascist mayor who held the job before him was run out of office as a collaborator. The people of Arezzo chose him.

Instead of giving food to a ravaged town, the Germans broke into all the stores and took everything away. Fra Raimondo scraped the countryside, begging for food and wine for the people, especially the poor. Before retreating to the hills, the enemy broke the water mains.

"Father, where will we get water?"

"Don't you remember the old well?" he reminded them. "It is near the abandoned farmhouse, on the road to Firenze." And the people went away happily to dig water from the earth.

When the wounded started to die from bombing injuries, he devoted three hours a day for medical treatment. He served as the physician, practicing skills he had picked up while comforting the sick in hospitals. Meantime, his friends, the partigani, would go about their daily jobs, carefully observing the movements of the enemy, passing the information along to the Americans.

The German commander of Arezzo discovered that the priest was helping the partisans, sheltering them in his abbey. Fra Raimondo was put up against the wall, facing a firing squad. But an Austrian lieutenant, who was a Catholic, saved his life, firmly declaring that no clergymen would be killed. The Austrian saved his life a second time when he was caught treating the wounded. But the partisans were executed.

Fra Raimondo passed along information to the Americans about the location of the German command post.

"If you will direct your artillery at that villa up on the hill, you'll hit them," he said.

That afternoon the villa and its occupants were destroyed.

To get closer to the action, I decided to attach myself to something called an "armored group" that consisted of a self-sufficient combat unit of tanks, artillery, engineers, and riflemen, because they were moving toward the battlefront.

The tanks churned up the dirt roads, turning them into slippery dust; it was like driving on glass. As I followed them, my jeep struck a rut, spun around, and tilted on a diagonal, carrying me halfway over the side. I washed and patched up a gash on my right leg (it's still visible) with my olive-drab pocket handkerchief, righted the jeep by putting it into reverse for traction, quickly shifted into the lowest forward gear, and continued following the tanks.

Our artillerymen appeared to be most active that afternoon. They maintained their franchise by firing harassing shells at German positions across the Arno. I dutifully wrote down their names and hometowns, listened to the battery commander explain his mission in stiff Army lingo combined with football plays—end runs and fake outs—and accepted the captain's invitation to try the armored group's mess for dinner.

What happened next was an example of the confusion that existed about the rank of *Stars and Stripes* correspondents. I noticed that two long tables were divided between field grade officers (majors to colonels) and company grade officers (captains and lieutenants). The colonel commanding the armored group invited me to sit with him and motioned the captain to sit with his ignoble kind. By the rules of the game, a lowly sergeant was not supposed to sit at either of these tables. One lieutenant-colonel, to be on the safe side, kept sirring me.

Finally, the colonel asked point-blank: "Are you fellows on *Stars and Stripes* civilians or soldiers?"

I mumbled something to the effect that we were soldiers but operated in the same way as civilian correspondents.

He pursued: "Then what's your rank?"

I replied: "Staff sergeant."

Nothing happened; the embarrassment was all mine.

I drove across the Arno over a Bailey bridge erected by our engineers. It was the only way to reach the other side of Florence. The Germans had dynamited every classical bridge—including the graceful Santa Trinita—with the exception of the Ponte Vecchio, which was too narrow and fragile to accommodate a tank. To express their contempt for the art-loving residents of Florence, whose museums they had looted, the enemy deliberately blew up the historic houses on both ends of the Ponte Vecchio, leaving behind mountains of rubble.

A shopkeeper cried when he showed me old postcards illustrating the Santa Trinita and the other beautiful bridges and Renaissance buildings along the riverfront before the Nazi barbarians destroyed them.

FLORENCE AN OPEN CITY—BUT ONLY TO NAZI ARTILLERY

By Sgt. Herbert Mitgang

FLORENCE—This Tuscan capital was an open city (meaning, not to be a military target) when the Allies were outside looking in. Today with the situation reversed, it is "open" to German artillery fire; the enemy doesn't give a damn about destroying Renaissance buildings and monuments that have no military significance.

When the German paratroop commander, General Fuchs, took over command of the Florence sector, his officers asked him how he planned to operate here. General Fuchs said: "To me, Florence and Smolensk are quite the same city." He referred to the Russian town that had been destroyed.

Allied Military Government officials are compiling a growing list of battered places of historic interest in this once-beautiful city. Last night, I was awakened by the sound of German shells falling on Florence. The Germans have shelled the city for the past week.

Before the Germans were booted out by the Allies, they took great pains to tell the world that they recognized the city was a center of great art and not a military objective. Their propaganda did not match the truth on the scene I witnessed. In the last ten days, 350 men, women, and children have been killed or severely wounded. Last Sunday, at 1130 hours, German guns dropped shells into a town square—just as church services were over.

The ancient Church of San Lorenzo was struck by seven artillery rounds and severely damaged. Before the Germans left, a venerable synagogue that they had used as a garage was deliberately ripped apart and its prayer books torched; the ornately carved doors holding the sacred Jewish Torahs were slashed with bayonets.

This is no atrocity story from some far-off place. These visible facts and deaths give greater credence to all the stories that sounded exaggerated. The Allied Military Government has established ten first-aid posts to take care of the casualties that are too heavy to handle in the hospitals. Allied medical personnel are helping the Florentines.

Museum curators were in tears describing the bomb damage done to the Ufizzi Art Gallery and the Strossi Palace. Works of art have been destroyed in the churches of San Lorenzo, Santa Maria Maggiore, Santa Spirito, and Santa Maria Novello. Most of the works by the great masters were removed by the Italians to places of safety. But, said an art expert, many priceless paintings and sculpture may soon be only masses of torn canvas and masses of plaster and marble.

A siren warning of an impending artillery attack would be unnecessary here. Florence today needs a mournful, tolling bell.

The first "battle" I saw was political: the battle on the walls between the political parties in anticipation of free elections. After two decades of Fascist rule, the people were expressing their preferences by painting the names of their parties—the Christian Democrats, Socialists, Communists, Action, and other independents—on the public buildings that had once carried only slogans urging them to work harder for the glory of Il Duce and his Fascist regime.

At one point as I wandered around the city's landmarks, I witnessed an amusing exchange between a British captain and an elderly woman who was a member of the romantic British colony that had set down roots in Tuscany at the time when Elizabeth and Robert Browning lived in Casa Guidi in the heart of Florence a century before.

"Captain," she said, recognizing his rank by the pips on his shoulder. "I am a British subject. The Germans have moved into my home in Fiesole and I'm afraid that they are going to steal my dishes and silverware. Would you please send a detachment of your men to safeguard my possessions?"

"Madam, I too am a British subject," the captain replied, "but I did not join His Majesty's Army in order to save your crockery. Good day."

I drove closer to the front lines where a company of Nisei was stationed. They were members of the most-decorated unit in the Army—the 442d Regimental Combat Team. (A future U.S. Senator, Daniel K. Inouye, served in the 442d.)

A Nisei lieutenant, noticing my *Stars and Stripes* insignia, told me, "Please don't call us Japanese-Americans. Most of us were born in California or Hawaii. We're children of immigrants— we're Nisei, which means second-generation in Japanese. You can call us Nisei or just plain Americans. We're here to prove that we're as American as anyone else."

As we talked a German .88 on the far side of an unnumbered hill fired a couple of rounds near us. I flinched; the Nisei soldiers did not. They continued to brew coffee for all of us and invited me to join them inside a cave in the mountainside.

The Nisei did not mention the fact that some members of their families were placed in detention camps in the United States. At that time, I didn't know much about that terrible injustice by the American government.

"Don't stand beneath that tree," one of the Nisei sergeants warned me. "If a shell hits the trunk or one of the big branches, it can rip the wood into small pieces of shrapnel." A German .88 was firing in our direction. A shell landed a few hundred yards away; too close for comfort.

Silently, out of the woods, an Italian partisan wearing brown-and-white golf shoes with spikes suddenly appeared, carrying a hunter's shotgun. He said he knew these mountains intimately and volunteered to shoot the Germans firing the .88 toward us. We greeted him as an ally.

Next, I witnessed a beautiful sight: the sporty-looking Italian partisan, a schoolteacher who taught in Florence, and a Nisei corporal, a fisherman from San Francisco in civilian life, carrying a Browning automatic rifle, teamed up and took off together in the direction of the enemy gun crew. (The scene has remained in my mind; after the war, I used it in a novel.)

Not more than a half-hour later, they both returned and gave us a thumbs-up. We gave them a V-for-Victory sign.

That was the last we heard from the .88.

My admiration for the partigani and the Nisei on that mountain outpost continued to grow in the next few days.

Our Nisei soldiers were great unhyphenated Americans.

When I returned to 5th Army Forward headquarters and filed a story, I struggled to describe what an .88 sounded like when a shell landed in your vicinity. I tried to find the right analogy, but all I could come up with was that it was like a train screeching to a stop on rusty railroad tracks.

After shaking the dust off my clothing, changing my socks, and washing out of my helmet, I quickly sacked out on a cot that was under canvas.

Early the next morning, I checked the latest location of our troops and the enemy forces at G-3 (Operations) and headed westward toward Pisa, which was partially under enemy control.

Naturally, I wanted to see the Leaning Tower, but I didn't want it to see me!

Which, in a way, was what happened—the damn Leaning Tower had eyes.

As I glanced across the Arno—which suddenly seemed more like a brook here than a wide river—toward the tower's upper stories, I saw two German soldiers in their gray coats looking directly at me and my jeep. One, with field glasses, obviously had me in his sights; the other held a field telephone to his ear.

If the Krauts wanted to shoot at me, I was in their sights—a lucky rifle shot away. I never felt as nakedly exposed in my life.

I turned off the main highway onto a small dirt road and headed for a small farmhouse, half-hidden behind a grove of trees, that I had been told was being used by our forward observers as a fire control center for div arty (division artillery).

To reach the farmhouse, you had to drive over an open stretch for about a quarter of a mile that gave the Germans in the Tower a clear view of anything that moved. The words on a crude hand-lettered sign at the beginning of the rutted road remain embedded in my mind:

SLOW TO
10 MILES
DUST RAISES SHELLS

Instinctively, I wanted to speed up and get to the semi-protection of the stone farmhouse quickly. But it would be a telltale sign to enemy artillerymen to fire at anything that raised a cloud of dust. As I crawled along, barely pressing the gas pedal, I watched the Germans moving between the narrow columns of the seven stories below the belfry.

In the farmhouse, the captain and his men invited me to share a cask of vino that they had liberated. A sergeant pointed to a large-scale map pinned to the wall. On the overlay, they had marked a rough rectangle that included the cathedral and the Leaning Tower. It was all church property—all designated as a no-fire zone. The letters OP (Observation Post) were clearly written over the Tower.

As evening fell and the level of wine in the cask lowered, talk turned (not for the first time, they said) to the idea of shooting down the Tower.

Our forward observers argued that the Germans surely knew the farmhouse was occupied—they were looking down our throats. We were well within the range of their .88s. Guided by their observers in the ancient Tower, enemy gunners held up the advance along this sector and, far worse, were causing some American casualties.

The top-ranking noncom here, a tech sergeant, didn't call it the Leaning Tower. Everyone knew what he meant when he said, "Let's shoot the fucker down! It's being used to kill our guys! And we can take out a couple of Nazis inside it at the same time!"

The captain and the sergeants theorized about where a well-placed hit would be most effective—on a low or a high floor. Could a single round bring down the whole shebang?

I listened in fascination.

What a story! To be present not at the creation but at the destruction of the world-famous landmark that had stood for some 800 years.

After dark, just when it looked as if the captain was persuaded to order a couple of rounds fired to bracket the target, the div arty colonel pulled up in his command car.

Almost immediately, looking at the men and the half-filled glasses of wine, he said, "I know what you're thinking, boys, but forget about it! The Tower is church property and we don't want to hand the Germans another Cassino to use as propaganda against us."

(The previous winter, American bombers had destroyed the monastery on the crest of Monte Cassino, causing an uproar around the world. It was a military foul-up. The ruins gave the Germans more than a propaganda victory; the rubble provided their troops better positions against the Allied infantrymen.)

The next day, after all of us had slept off the effects of the emptied cask of vino, the Germans began to retreat toward new positions in the Apennines, which they called the Gothic line.

I crossed the Arno and headed for the Leaning Tower. I noticed that the enemy's signal wire was still hanging down from one of the upper floors. It was the proof I was looking for to confirm what I had seen; the Germans used it as an OP. I reported my findings to 5th Army Operations to get it on record that the Germans occupied church property for military purposes. Then I filed my story about the city's liberation.

PISA SHATTERED AND GHOSTLY

By Sgt. Herbert Mitgang

WITH THE 5TH ARMY—Pisa is spooky this morning.

A stiff wind spirals through the shells that once were houses, creaking the shutters of Pisa. Further down the strada leading to the historic cathedral and Tower, a rain pipe drips pieces of wet plaster on a bomb crater, breaking the stillness of an early dawn.

Telephone wires crisscross in and out of the strewn tram tracks forming almost natural tank barriers. A mountain of rubble—brick, wood, and steel—blocks the avenues of approach to the famous monuments. Bedrooms, those whose inner secrets were once so well kept, have become public eyefuls.

A lean-faced municipal fireman stumbles toward this soldier–correspondent and warns him not to turn the corner because a shot was just fired from that tall factory building. The fireman's scalp is cut and pockmarks of blood are running down his eyebrows and under his nostrils.

From a store that once sold women's undergarments, a captain from a tank destroyer outfit signals to one of his men and when he whispers something in the soldier's ear they both giggle. A moment later the soldier jams a fresh clip into his carbine and starts up the street, slowly inching his way along the smashed sidewalk. He turns the corner and suddenly two shots are fired in our direction.

Winding through a narrow alleyway, I still see the German "Achtung Minen" signs. This is no place to take a misstep.

But the church buildings are untouched. However, I notice a small chip on the Tower facing the former German side of the Arno.

In an art works shop in the cathedral area, there are hundreds of alabaster reproductions of the Leaning Tower—from eight inches to four feet tall—for sale. American soldiers in for a souvenir kill snatch up the small ones at 25 lire a copy.

There are dozens of people coming out of the broken buildings. Sleepy-eyed mothers come up to my jeep and hold up their hungry children. I am happy to be able to pass them boxes of my K rations. I am told that the Germans never shared their food with the people. One woman who speaks English keeps repeating to me, "God bless you."

As I try to break away from the crowds, they applaud and shout, "Americano! Viva United States!"

In the church there are a few hundred families. On the altars kids are stretched out on blankets, sleeping away their hunger. They have lived in this no-fire zone for weeks. On the church steps two young signorine are washing clothes, using the rough steps instead of soap.

Everyone has a story to tell.

Six Jews and four Christians were placed in a room with the door barred. Then a Hun broke the window and one of his Nazi brothers threw a hand grenade inside. Everybody died. An entire Jewish family, including women and children, was killed with a machine pistol by a German colonel. Jews and Gentiles alike were burned to death by flamethrowers.

An American lieutenant inquired whether there were any watches, cameras, or binoculars for sale. The civilians told him that two weeks ago Germans came up to them and politely asked for the time of day. When an Italian pulled out his watch, the German took it.

On the way out of town, past the shattered remains of the birthplace of Galileo, I stopped at a house that was once used by the SS as an officers' club. There were some lewd murals on the walls. Over the entrance, a German sign read: "Remember wherever you are or whatever you do, you are members of the SS."

After I bought a small reproduction of the Leaning Tower, there was only one more thing left for me to do: Climb the real Tower. An old caretaker unlocked the doorway, and I became the first Allied correspondent to ascend the 294 steps to the belfry.

Gazing over the lovely Pisan countryside, I was glad that I never had to write that big story of the tower's demise.

After Pisa was captured, I decided to accompany the 92d Infantry Division—the first African American division to go into combat in Italy—on the western sector leading to the northern industrial cities. They were nicknamed the "Buffalo soldiers" and mostly were commanded by white senior officers.

I sat down next to a white captain and asked him: How do you think your men are going to do in action?

The captain replied: "I've been with them since we trained together in the States. They're good at drilling because they've got natural-born rhythm, but I'm afraid they won't stand up in combat."

"Have you ever been in combat, Captain?"

"No," he said.

Of course, I did not write anything about his prejudiced comments.

After speaking to many of the African American enlisted men, the headline over my article summed up a little of what I wanted to say about racism.

MEN OF 92D ARE ANXIOUS TO FIGHT RACE-HATING NAZIS

By Sgt. Herbert Mitgang

The first impression of the 92d Infantry Division, now a part of the 5th Army, is the one that sticks. These Negro enlisted men, led by both white and Negro officers, are eager to close with the enemy.

They know the Hitler gang and what they stand for. They are enthusiastic because, like many other people, they have a personal score to settle against the forces of racial or religious intolerance.

Like any other American division the men come from all over the United States and every walk of life. Most of the non-commissioned officers graduated from specialist training schools. The cadre includes one private who was bucking for his Doctor of Philosophy degree before he enlisted. All but one of the Negro lieutenants and captains came up through the ranks and attended officers' training school.

The division was activated on Oct. 15, 1942. At that time they were at Camp Breckinridge, in Kentucky. Then they trained in the Arizona desert. They took part in the Louisiana maneuvers. Next stop: Naples.

Shortly thereafter, they headed for the front.

The medics in the 92d Division are made up of Negro doctors, with the exception of two surgeons.

In World War I, the 92d was activated at Fort Riley, Kansas. The division saw service with the AEF, especially in the Argonne campaign.

Before they moved into the line in Italy, Lt. Gen Mark W. Clark, 5th Army commander told the men: "You have a chance to cover yourself with glory."

"That's just what we're going to do," a staff sergeant told me, "now that we're getting a chance to fight those racist Nazis."

HEPPED-UP 92D MOVES GRIMLY UPON NAZI GOTHIC LINE

By Sgt. Herbert Mitgang

WITH THE 92D DIVISION, Sept. 1 [1944]—Three hepped-up battalions of the 5th Army's Negro division last night and this morning forded and waded across the River Arno. The fight to crack the Gothic Line has begun, led in this sector by Negro infantrymen who made the first crossing in strength.

The 92d has already reached its first objective, and forward reconnaissance patrols are eagerly pushing ahead. German resistance was light all along the front although land mines and isolated pockets of snipers have been encountered. Engineers of the First Armored Division are sweeping the northern lanes over the river while strong tank, tank destroyer, and infantry also are fording the Arno.

The offensive started last night when three patrols in company strength sloshed through the mud and shallow waters all during the day. The three battalions, commanded by Maj. J. Herrara, Texas; Capt. H. Price, Oklahoma, and Col. C. Daugette, Alabama, followed up to establish strong bridgeheads.

They are now firmly in possession of the area from La Rotta to Cascina, and have penetrated one mile across the river.

The first battalion this morning encircled a house that sheltered enemy snipers and wiped out all harassing fire. In this action, two casualties were reported and two Nazis were captured. One Pole who was captured said he had thrown away his gun last July and said he was not at war with anybody; he was sent to a prisoner-of-war cage.

Pfc. John H. Temple, Raleigh, N.C., the driver for an operations officer, said, "All the men were sure happy to be in on the attack."

Lt. Lawrence D. Spencer, Elizabeth, N.J., a Negro platoon leader, was photographed interrogating a captured German officer. It made a perfect picture: a so-called Nazi superman who was a captive of a black American soldier.

I half lucked-out on one story: Prime Minister Winston Churchill visited 5th Army Forward headquarters while I was there. But I was too shy and inexperienced at that time to seek a private interview with him. Instead, I filed a straightforward piece about the great man's visit:

CHURCHILL (AND CIGAR) VISIT 5TH

By Sgt. Herbert Mitgang

WITH THE 5TH ARMY—Prime Minister Winston Churchill today told thousands of 5th Army soldiers that together with the British 8th Army they would play "an absolutely vital part in the long, hard struggle which lies ahead." He predicted "great things" for the men who fought the enemy together in the Italian campaign.

Wearing a sun helmet and continually puffing and chewing one of his traditionally long cigars, the Prime Minister was given a tremendous ovation from the time he stepped out of the personal plane of General Sir Harold Alexander early this morning until he departed for an unknown destination in the afternoon.

Lt. Gen. Mark W. Clark, the 5th's commander, conducted Mr. Churchill on a tour of the front lines around the Arno River. He pulled the lanyard on a 240-mm gun against two medium enemy guns north of Pisa. The shell fell 200 yards short but two rounds later, an air artillery observer noted direct hits.

Mr. Churchill spoke to members of the 34th Division, 5th Army Wacs and nurses, and members of the Brazilian Expeditionary Force. It was a big day for Italian civilians who greeted him all along the route. He returned their ovation with a V-for-Victory salute.

From General Clark he received the British flag that was raised in Rome the night of the city's capture. "This is the first Allied flag to fly in a captured enemy capital," said General Clark.

During his inspection, Mr. Churchill spoke to many soldiers. He stopped before T-Sgt. Frederick Uccelina, Norwalk, Conn., and asked him about his Purple Heart ribbon.

"Churchill asked me if I was all right now," Sergeant Uccelina said, "and when I told him I was, he said, 'Good boy.'"

CHAPTER 12

Corsica

The French Underground

FREE FRENCH friends at Allied Force Headquarters told me that the Maquis (the Resistance or Underground, as it was also called) was active on the French island of Corsica in the Mediterranean. I decided to see the Corsicans who were sabotaging the German forces there. So I hopped a ride on a hospital plane that was outfitted with cots to transport wounded members of the Maquis back to Algiers for medical treatment.

In Ajaccio and out in the countryside, I spent time with the Corsican patriots fighting the enemy forces who were in retreat on the northern end of the island. After a week of interviews and observations, I returned with enough material for several stories. When I told Herbert L. Matthews, the chief *New York Times* correspondent, what I had seen and heard, he urged me to write an article for *The Times Magazine*, because no reporter had explained the inner workings of the French Underground on Corsica or on the Continent.

I was greatly pleased when Matthews, the most respected American foreign correspondent in the Mediterranean Theater of Operations, thought my work was good enough to appear in his newspaper. (Matthews was revered for his coverage of the anti-Franco Loyalists during the Spanish Civil War; Ernest Hemingway called him the bravest reporter in Spain. Later, he exposed the murderous practices of the Fascists; Mussolini placed him under house arrest in Italy.)

It took me about a week of nights to write the article on my portable Remington. I was in awe, more than a little scared, realizing that I was writing for possible publication in *The New York Times*.

Herb Matthews glanced at the article, nodded approval, and immediately dispatched it to *The Times Magazine*.

Here is how it appeared there on January 4, 1944—exactly as I had written it—without a single change in the text. The sub-heads below the main headline were added in New York.

A SHADOW ARMY LEAPS TO ARMS

The drama enacted in Corsica will be repeated in many other lands.

That invisible French army—the Underground—awaits the day of reckoning with the Nazi invaders. Already it has struck telling blows in Corsica. An American soldier tells how it operated on that island. —Sgt. Herbert Mitgang, *Stars and Stripes* staff

Ajaccio, Corsica—Those were the long days, the long hours, when Corsica's citizen army looked seaward, patiently waited. That was the time, seven days after United States troops clambered up the beaches of North Africa. Then the yellow rag paper tracts were secretly passed hand-to-hand among the faithful, ever watchful of the Germans.

This was to be the lesson, the proving ground for Europe's patriots: below, liberation for French North Africa was accomplished; flanked by Italy and its Mediterranean possessions, Corsica watched its own shores, waited for Allied landings and freedom.

In 14-pt handset type on hand-ripped slips of paper, islanders read a secret message:

State of Alarm

On his posters the enemy has clearly indicated the activities which hinder him since the debarkation; he has warned us under the threat of death. But it is the Homeland we must obey and not the enemy—our future prisoners. France counts on everyone to do his duty. Every evening at 2250 hours listen to the broadcast over Radio France (Algiers) for Corsica.

NATIONAL FRONT.

And the clandestine radios, in homes watched by Italians, Germans, and Corsican gauleiters, picked up innocent-sounding news broadcasts from Radio France which directed their movements in coordination with the temporary government set up in Algiers.

In a small mountain town in the northeastern region, Jacques Manachem, a 29-year-old newspaperman, sat pounding the keys of a typewriter. A former photographer for *Paris Soir*, his work had taken him to London for several years and to Hollywood for three months. He was by no means handsome. His reddish-brown hair topped a plain-looking face, but his body appeared sturdy, with long, wiry strength. Only his eyes looked unusual. They had a quick, darting glance that spotted everyone who walked into the Fascist headquarters in the town.

The Fascists were unaware of him. On their own official stationery, he transmitted secret messages in code and passed them along from province to province, covering the entire island.

The patriots worked in units of five, patterned after the citizens' army in France; they numbered many French evacuees in their group. The principal reason for the compact units was security. Composed as they were, if one man was caught and tortured to give information, he could reveal only four others.

Of the five original leaders in Corsica, three were members of the Communist party. Each original member carefully chose five others, and they, in turn picked out others. This went on, town to town, until 15,000 men were patriot "regulars." One-third of the men capable of bearing arms were in this partisan army.

They met in deserted farmhouses and barns; in mountain caves known only to people who lived in the region all of their lives; in innocent-looking taverns. The men lived spartan lives. They had to. It was either self-denial or pitiless persecution if discovered. Organization was more absolute than in a regular army, and there was no such thing as questioning or disobeying an order. In the hearts of the men in every unit were engraved these vows, similar to those taken by their brother patriots hiding deep in the forests of France:

1. You are not only fugitives, you are also soldiers.
2. Hold no communication with family or friends.
3. Do not complain if your family cannot help you.
4. You expect no pay.
5. There is no distinction in the ranks between race, faith, or party.
6. Never abandon a wounded comrade.
7. Care for and protect your arms.

And they kept their allegiance. The British Royal Air
Force, in the meantime, supplied the patriots with arms. In
close cooperation with Radio France in Algiers, codes were
broadcast which gave the time and location when and where
rifles and ammunition would be parachuted down from an
Allied plane.

"We like good apples" might mean "Tonight at Ajaccio,
usual spot, usual signal." There was plenty of trouble, plenty
of slip-ups, between code signals and final delivery. One
evening a religious feast was going on in an east coast village.
Festive lights shone brightly in many homes. The Fascist gar-
rison in the village silently tolerated the feast. That night an
RAF plane swooped down over the town, and saw the lights.
The pilot thought they were his signal. Bundles of small arms
floated earthward and plopped down in the public square. The
precious arms cost lives that night—Italian and patriot—before
they were partially retrieved and secreted away.

By this time, German, Italian, and French police were on
the trail of Jacques Manachem. He had revealed himself as a
unit leader. Meanwhile, high back in the mountains, Jacques
was editing *Le Patriote*, organ of the Corsican National Front,
binding force for every woman and man on the island. Five
thousand copies of the quarter-sized paper were secretly passed
from hand to hand. As far north as Bastia, an Italian truck driven by a patriot distributed the people's paper.

A dozen or more times suspicious enemy soldiers combed
the forest attempting to find the hidden presses. Once Italian
police into whose hands the newspaper had fallen entered the
very area where Jacques was busily engaged printing an edition.
He silenced the whir of the presses and waited to be caught,
breathlessly. The police were no more than three feet from him,
but they did not discover the hideout. For this hilltop land was
the "maquis"—the peculiar terrain of Corsica where the trees

and scrub bushes are like jungles—where one unfamiliar with it cannot see three feet ahead

False names were assigned to members of the patriot units to prevent detection. "Remington" was the name for one clerk who used the European model of that typewriter. "Hannibal" was the code for another.

Sept. 9, 1943, will go down in Corsican history alongside July 14, 1789. That was the day the Americans moved into Ajaccio in force, together with their French and British allies. The patriots were ready. They were familiar with the roads to the Ligurian Sea. They knew the German strategy was to head north, toward Bastia, and escape.

For six crucial days the Germans were delayed in their flight by the patriots. The hated Boche were cut off on the western coast, but the patriots' machine guns were no real match for the Nazi tanks and artillery pieces hastily cutting across the Tyrrhenian Sea side of the island. Wherever small companies were trapped, however, they were annihilated or taken prisoner— mostly they were killed. The patriots counted 500 of their own dead after the battles.

At two o'clock in the afternoon when most of the Germans were driven off the island, life returned to the capital city, Ajaccio. Flags were draped over the balustrades. Crowds of mountain warriors, armed with the weapons they had carefully nurtured and successfully used, marched fearlessly down the Cours Grandval, down toward Napoleon's statue. Their clothes were ragged, they were out of step—but they were soldiers.

Jacques Manachem stood in the doorway at 14 Cours Grandval, watching as the men walked by, singing and joking. *Le Patriote*, now with the largest circulation on the island, and no longer printed in the "maquis," was still proudly edited by him. He was one of them. He had helped to free his homeland.

Late that night, the celebration over, the youthful editor sat at his cluttered desk and penned the next day's editorial:

"These men, these people—one doesn't have to teach them liberty or government. They discovered what they wanted, what free government was, when they united against forced rule. Their elections in case of death came from the bottom; went from town to town—were not dictated from above. They had representative government in their people's army.

"When the crisis was at hand there was no question of politics. There was only a goal of freedom for the living, a new hope for those yet unborn. We have only a small island. There are patriots now fighting all over Europe, risking their lives under threat of death, pursued like thieves and murderers. They, too, know what liberty means.

These citizen-patriots must have their chance."

Some years after the end of the war, I tried to track down Jacques Manachem and discovered that he had immigrated to the new State of Israel.

CHAPTER 13

New York

The Home Front

ARLY IN 1945, Lt. Col. Bob Neville asked Bill Hogan and me if we would like to go back to New York for three months to work for Army News Service and also to write about the home front for our Mediterranean edition of *Stripes*.

Bob seriously said, "You won't find New York as much fun as Rome. You'll be glad to return here."

But after being overseas for close to three years, Bill and I jumped at the chance to go home

And so I became what we called a "reverse foreign correspondent" in an unfamiliar place—the United States.

We flew home in an unarmed four-engine bomber (a B-24) that had been converted into a transport plane, sitting on cold bucket seats. The first stop was Casablanca, then on to the Azores, where the plane refueled and we stretched our legs. At the PX in the Azores, I bought a Modern Library edition of Russian short stories. Reading the book across the Atlantic, I became familiar with that humane literature for the first time; it was so different from Socialist realism. Our happy landfall in North America was in Newfoundland.

After arriving in New York, we gave the Air Corps pilot a dollar bill to sign. This made us what was known as a "short snorter." ("Long snorters" flew across the Pacific Ocean.) It was still unusual in those days to fly the oceans; if you boasted that you had done so, you had to show your signed dollar bill or pay for the drinks.

When I stepped off the plane in New York, a strange thing happened: I was afraid to walk on the grass. If you had once been in former enemy-held territory in Italy, you learned to stay inside the tapes that showed where our combat engineers had cleared the mines and it was safe to walk. That feeling of caution lasted for about a month.

I hopped a taxi that took me home to Brooklyn, where my mother and father and two younger sisters (who had become volunteer nurse's aides) were waiting, joyful tears at the ready. We sat down to a big dinner together that included real chicken soup and flanken, two of my mother's specialties.

Then I borrowed my father's Pontiac, and drove over to Shirley's house. She looked even more beautiful than her photograph that I had kept in my room in Rome.

After a few days at home, I reported to the Army News Service office in the Bartholomew building on 42nd Street off Third Avenue, across the street from the *New York Daily News*. After checking in with a few administrative brass hats, I was told that I would be entitled to a big $3 per diem for meals and any out-of-pocket expenses. I was assigned a desk and typewriter, handed a batch of national newspapers and wire-service dispatches and told to put together stories that would be sent to all military publications, including *The Stars and Stripes*. No one looked over my copy; I could write whatever interested me.

Bill Hogan had a good news story to pursue in his San Francisco hometown: the United Nations was coming into existence there. He filed several fine pieces about the founding of the U.N. After visiting for a few weeks with his family and friends at his old newspaper, the *San Francisco Chronicle*, Bill returned to New York. Together, we ground out stateside news for Army News Service, dropped into the *Stripes* office downstairs to learn what was going on back in Rome—which we considered our overseas home—and to read the latest copies of the Mediterranean edition.

Eventually, the Army brass hats caught up with its hotshot "reverse foreign correspondents." Together with staffers from *Yank*, the Army weekly magazine, which had offices in the same building, Bill Hogan and I were told that we had to do calisthenics. In ragged formation one day a week, we marched up Third Avenue to a YMCA that was a few blocks away, while civilians stared at a curious group of out-of-shape soldiers. At the Y, we were given Judo lessons. Marching back to our building, which was nicknamed "Fort Bartholomew," some of us peeled off at Tim Costello's newspapermen's bar for a beer.

I had one sad story to write: the death of President Roosevelt and the reaction of the American people. F.D.R. was the only President most of us had ever known—his New Deal had pulled the country out of the Depression and, while sitting in a wheelchair in the White House, he served as our wartime commander-in-chief.

The best event of all that spring was personal: Shirley and I were married on May 13, 1945. It was the wisest decision of my life. We had exchanged hundreds of letters while I was overseas and learned about each other's personalities and dreams.

Germany had surrendered a few days before our marriage. My tenure with Army News Service continued; theoretically, I was still obliged to return to *Stripes* in Rome.

The war continued against Japan. We knew nothing about the atom bombs when they were dropped on Hiroshima and Nagasaki. Since then, questions have rightfully been raised about the morality of bombing populated cities. But I remember our reaction at the time:

First, we were glad that the United States and not Germany had developed the terrible nuclear weapon. Otherwise, Hitler would have incinerated London and New York.

Second, the nuclear bomb meant that Japan would soon have to surrender and we wouldn't have to be shipped to the Pacific to fight, or even to write, again.

Friends began returning to the States and we had many reunions in New York. At a memorable party at Marion and Irwin Shaw's apartment on the Upper East Side, I introduced Shirley as my wife.

"I see you married that girl you were going with in Algiers," Irwin wisecracked.

Among the guests at the party were the legendary Bill Estoff, the *Stripes* circulation manager, with whom I had stayed at Maria's happy place in Naples, and his wife, Ede, who also was from Syracuse. Several *New Yorker* writers were there, including Joe Mitchell and Joe Liebling. I overheard them kidding each other about who owed the magazine more money (or words) on their drawing accounts.

While still in uniform in New York, Bill Hogan and I hit the jackpot. Bill Mauldin had sold his book, *Up Front*, to Universal-International Pictures in Hollywood. The studio said it needed a screen treatment, and Mauldin recommended Hogan, Dave Golding (who was still in Rome; he mailed us cinematic suggestions), and me for the job.

Bill Hogan and I worked together in my apartment, fashioning Mauldin's brilliant captions into a story and dialogue. We included some of our favorite drawings from the book and from *Stripes*. My favorite showed two young officers overlooking a sunset in southern France. One says to the other: "Beautiful view. Is there one for the enlisted men?"

What we tried to do was convey Mauldin's affection for the enlisted men serving in the front lines and his elusive sardonic quality that went beyond humor. He wasn't always joking.

We were hired for six weeks. Every week Hogan and I showed up at the Universal office in Rockefeller Center and turned in our material.

The treasurer, who was related to the studio head, handed us our weekly checks. As she did so, she invariably said, "I bet you boys never saw money like this before."

True enough—we were still "boys" (no gray hairs yet). And we were making more than sergeant's pay.

Some months later, our screen treatment and other material was used by the two distinguished Lardner brothers, John and Ring, Jr., when they created an original screenplay. *Up Front* eventually became a movie starring two important actors, Tom

Ewell and David Wayne, playing Bill Mauldin's two memorable characters, Willie and Joe.

Shirley and I enjoyed living in Manhattan after growing up and attending schools in Brooklyn.

One evening, Bill Hogan joined us for a roast beef dinner at the Palm restaurant on Second Avenue. When we asked for the check, the waiter pointed to a stranger at a nearby table and said, "That gentleman insisted on paying for your dinners." We got up and thanked him. The stranger pointed to the hash marks on our sleeves. "I see you guys have served overseas," he said. "I wanted to thank you."

After that festive dinner, Shirley, Bill, and I strolled along Fifth and Park Avenues. Observant as usual, Bill listened to the whistles of doormen summoning taxis and pointed at the majestic towers of Manhattan.

When we stood on the parapet on 57th Street, overlooking the East River and the Manhattan skyline, Bill declared that it all reminded him of a Hollywood movie set. He commented: "Are you getting this down, Mannie?"

It was a line we repeated to each other for years while visiting each other in California and New York.

After VE-Day came VJ-Day, and suddenly World War II was over. I did not have to return to Army News Service or to *Stars and Stripes* in Rome.

If you had enough of what was called "points," you could be discharged early. In addition to overseas service, I had "points" for campaigns in North Africa, Sicily, and Italy, plus for aerial combat—adding up to more than enough to be separated from the service. Together with some friends from *Yank* magazine, I was discharged from the Army at Fort Dix, New Jersey, in that lovely summer of 1945. I was handed a Good Conduct medal, a European Victory medal, and a ribbon that entitled me to wear six "battle stars," for the various campaigns, though I hardly considered myself a warrior either in the Air Corps or on *Stars and Stripes.*

And so I became a civilian again. One of the final things I had had to do when I was discharged was to write down my occupation. I wondered: Is this for World War III? If so, I wanted my same military job.

When I had enlisted, I had written: LAWYER.

Now, unhesitatingly, I wrote: REPORTER.

CHAPTER 14

Newspaperman
and Author

RETURNING TO civilian live at the age of 25, and happily married, I had to decide on a career.

Although I was interested in the law in a general way—especially constitutional law—I had no desire to hang out a shingle and serve commercial corporations. My instincts told me that I should make a living by my pen (or typewriter), if I could. That meant being a newspaperman.

Without a job, I went around to the offices of the New York Newspaper Guild and said that I'd like to join the Guild, the union that represented reporters, editors, and commercial workers. I admitted that practically my only newspaper experience was serving on *The Stars and Stripes*. After paying a modest fee, I was handed a Guild card and signed up as an "unemployed newspaperman."

Because I had written a couple of pieces for the *New York Times* from overseas, I decided to apply there first. Actually, ex-Lt.

Jim Burchard, with whom I had worked in Algiers and Palermo, first offered to get me a job as a sports writer on his paper, *The World Telegram*, but I was no longer interested in sports exclusively. Friends at the *Times* told me that the best place to apply was the Sunday Department, which put out the *Times Magazine*, Book Review, News of the Week in Review, and other special sections.

I got an interview with one of the assistant Sunday editors, Francis Brown, who said that they always were looking for good "deskmen"—a Guild category.

"This is a special department," he said. "Our standards are even higher than those on the daily paper. What makes you think you can write for the Sunday *Times*?"

I showed him a clipping of my article on the French Maquis from the *Magazine* that Herbert L. Matthews had encouraged me to write and also a piece I had done for the Week in Review about combat in Tuscany.

Brownie (as everyone called him) seemed impressed and set me up for an interview with Lester Markel, the notoriously tough-minded Sunday editor. Mr. Markel remembered my *Magazine* article and said that he could use another deskman. The main thing he wanted from me wash fresh ideas. He said that I would be the first veteran on his staff and offered me a job paying the regular Guild minimum. Then he told me to report to work the following Monday.

I rushed home to tell Shirley that I had landed a job at the *New York Times*!

And so, on the first Monday in November 1945, I was greeted by the head of the Sunday Department copydesk, L. V. Updegraff ("Call me Uppy"), an elderly gentleman. After assigning me a desk, he introduced me to some of the other copyeditors. Among these old-timers was a former Liberal Democrat of the British Parliament and a former reporter who had covered Charles Lindbergh's solo flight to Paris. My desk was next to a charming woman, Margaret Farrar, the pioneering editor of the *Magazine*'s crossword puzzle. I was the youngest deskman on the Sunday staff.

Uppy gave me an education in big-time editing. Fancy writing was deplored. The most important thing was accuracy—by the book, meaning the *Times Stylebook*, which he had helped to edit. I learned that he had been in the class ahead of Sinclair (Red) Lewis at Yale, and had marked Lewis's English papers. "He could never write," Uppy told me about the first American to be awarded the Nobel Prize in Literature. Uppy, a classics scholar, was always reading the Greeks and Romans. If he ever saw me carrying a modern novel, he'd say, "Oh, are you up to the twentieth century already?" Sometimes we'd spend fifteen minutes discussing whether a foreign word required a circumflex, acute, or grave accent. He kept his own foreign dictionaries in the deep drawer of his desk, locked up at night. Accuracy demanded documentation—in writing. Once, when he challenged me about the royal title of a member of the House of Lords, I replied, "I just called and checked with the British Information Service." Not good enough; not in writing. He had a personal subscription to Hansard's Parliamentary Reports; no Baron was ever called an Earl by mistake after Uppy double-checked my editing.

I particularly enjoyed reading the cables from our renowned foreign correspondents—among them Drew Middleton, Clifton Daniel, Herbert L. Matthews (my friend in Rome). I wielded a thick copyreader's pencil, but, other than fixing errors of transmission and marking paragraphs, the old pros required very little editing. I also liked writing headlines that summarized the substance of a lengthy dispatch in a few words. I learned the word counts of the various *Times* typefaces (Bookman, Karnak, Latin Condensed, etc.)—everything but Bodoni Bold, the handsome type used in the *New York Herald Tribune*, our rival paper that emphasized lively feature writing (later known as the "new journalism"). If I returned late to my desk after too leisurely a lunch hour, Uppy, a gentle taskmaster, would mete me out an obvious punishment. Instead of a juicy cable, he gave me garden copy or the bridge column to edit. Since I didn't know bridge I passed the column over to John Willig, a bridge player. Willig, who had been *The Stars and Stripes* magazine editor in Rome, also had joined the *Sunday Magazine*, untangling articles by academics. As a reward for this difficult labor, he inherited the job of Men's Fashion section editor, which included an annual photographing junket to Palm Beach. Other *Stars and Stripes* companions were on the paper, including Howard Taubman, Jack Raymond, John Radosta, Hilary Lyons, Sherman Davis, and a few printers.

After a couple of years of learning the standards of being a Sunday deskman, I was drafted by John B. Oakes, the editor of the Week in Review section, to be his assistant. Oakes, a former Rhodes Scholar, had risen to be a lieutenant colonel in the Office of Strategic Services during the war. An experienced newspaperman, he had been a reporter for the *Washington Post*. His special interest was conservation and the environment. John became my benefactor on the *Times* and a good friend for life.

Among my tasks on the Week in Review was making up the pages and working with the printers in the composing room. I had learned how to do just that in newspaper plants in North Africa and Italy—how to read the type upside down and backwards on my side of the printing stone; how to cut and revise pieces to make them fit; how to rewrite headlines; and how to beg linotypists to make my corrections quickly to meet our early Saturday deadlines. I enjoyed the mechanics of producing a newspaper.

The *New York Times* Book Review section was part of the Sunday Department. Many war novels and memoirs were beginning to be published. John K. Hutchens, the Book Review editor, gave me a steady flow of books to review. One of the daily book critics, Charles Poore, asked me to fill in for him during his summer vacation. That meant two reviews a week. He called me "Sergente" and I called him "Capitano." We met in Palermo, where he served as a captain in the Allied Military Government.

I was allowed to select my own books for daily reviews. Because of my stint in Italy, I reviewed many Italian and other European novelists; they became one of my specialties in the daily and Sunday Book Review.

The most important book I reviewed over the next few years when I became a regular standby critic was Michael Harrington's *The Other America*, which exposed the struggle and dire living conditions of one-third of America's families. I was later told that the book was read in the White House and inspired the government's War on Poverty.

Like many of my newspaper colleagues, I thought that I should try to write a novel. Aware that my only experience was in nonfiction writing and editing, I decided to learn a little about a new craft. I signed up for a one-night-a-week course in fiction writing at Columbia University's School of General Studies.

When I told my close wartime friend Bill Hogan, by then the literary editor of the *San Francisco Chronicle*, that I hoped to write a novel, he advised, "Don't quit your day job."

★ ★ ★

Writing at home before going to work and on weekends, I began my first novel, *The Return*. I drew on my wartime background for much of the story, which almost all takes place in Sicily. It was published by Simon & Schuster, received good reviews, and was reissued several times in paperback editions.

After some years on the Week in Review, I was given a section of my own to edit by the Sunday editor. I became the supervising editor of the Sunday Drama section (now called Arts and Leisure). This section covered all the performing arts. The first page invariably included a beautiful line drawing by Al Hirschfeld and a theater essay by Brooks Atkinson—the finest critic, in any field, in New York. He encouraged the growth of Off Broadway. To read Atkinson was a lesson in fairness and elegant writing. I felt honored to be in his presence.

I also watched with admiration and encouraged Jack Gould, the leading television critic in the nation, who was feared by the commercial networks because he exposed their ratings-driven drivel. He advocated the development of public television.

Because of changes taking place at the *Times*, as well as at CBS News, I accepted an offer to join the network's news department. I was given a newly created title: assistant to the president and executive editor.

Early on, I changed the nature of my job, deemphasizing its administrative duties and concentrating on writing and producing documentary films. These were to include *D-Day plus 20 Years: Eisenhower Returns to Normandy*, with Walter Cronkite as correspondent; *Carl Sandburg at Gettysburg* and *Carl Sandburg: Lincoln's Prairie Years*, both with correspondent Howard K. Smith; *Henry Moore: Man of Form*, with correspondent Charles Collingwood; *Anthony Eden on Vietnam*, again with correspondent Collingwood; and *Ben-Gurion on the Bible*, with correspondent Alexander Kendrick. I also worked with Eric Sevareid, the erudite correspondent, helping with political analysis during elections.

It was during the Vietnam War that I did the work that engaged me most deeply. I decided to go to Saigon to see for myself how our coverage could be improved. It was handled well by the battlefield reporters—among them Morley Safer, Peter Arnett, and Dan Rather—but I felt there was a lack of analysis and that the Pentagon was calling the shots.

While in Vietnam, I flew in an armed helicopter that came under fire to visit a battalion from the First Infantry Division near the Cambodian frontier. I had observed the division in North Africa and Sicily.

Later, in Saigon, I reunited with two outstanding *Stars and Stripes* (Mediterranean) combat correspondents, Jack Foisie of the *Los Angeles Times* and Stanley Swinton of the Associated Press. In Jack's apartment, we waxed nostalgic about a good war—World War II.

Back in New York, I wrote a long report that called for the need to have a senior correspondent doing analytical reports about the war that went beyond the battlefield. I had learned that Vietnam was also a political, economic, and religious war. And I helped initiate a series of in-depth programs called "Vietnam Perspective" to give voice to views opposed to the escalation of the war.

I left CBS News after three long years. I had come to realize that television news was not a writer's medium and its management demands were not for me.

That is why I was delighted to get a call from John Oakes, by then editor of the Editorial Page, asking me to return to the *New York Times* as a member of his Editorial Board. He wanted me to help him start the Op Ed page; I became its deputy editor. It was a trailblazing assignment. During my tenure, every Nobel laureate in literature was invited to write for the page. Soon other newspapers all over the United States copied our Op Ed page.

As a member of the Editorial Board, I wrote editorials and occasional signed columns on domestic and sometimes foreign issues. My special fields were constitutional rights, civil rights, the law and court reform, gun control, the federal regulatory agencies, American history, and the arts and humanities. I pushed hard for the creation of the Corporation for Public Broadcasting and the Public Broadcasting Service (PBS), knowing they were needed to supplement the commercial networks.

The happiest and most fruitful time of my life at the *Times* was the eleven years I spent writing editorials. A lot was happening in the United States and in the world in the 1960s and 1970s, including the civil rights revolution and the Vietnam War. I had my say against the "march of folly" (as my friend, historian Barbara Tuchman, called our role in Vietnam), with its human carnage on both sides.

A major, unwanted changed occurred in my career at the *Times* in 1976. There was a palace revolution and Oakes was replaced as the editor of the liberal Editorial Page and so were most of his editorial writers.

I was given the option of another assignment. I was asked by the publisher to remain on the paper. A new job was created for me to match my interests in literature.

And so, I was appointed the first publishing correspondent of the *Times*. This meant writing two columns a week—one every Friday in the arts pages and another for the Sunday Book Review section.

It came at an interesting time in American publishing. Some of the traditional publishing houses were merging and some were being acquired by foreign conglomerates. These changes often were—and continue to be—page one news.

As publishing correspondent, I traveled all over the country and attended the book fairs in Frankfurt and Jerusalem a number of times. I was greatly interested in the work of small and independent publishing houses.

Wherever I went, I interviewed authors—Rebecca West and Eric Ambler in London, Vladimir Nabokov in Montreux, Gunter Grass in Berlin, Samuel Beckett in Paris, Sean O'Faolain in Dublin, Georges Simenon in Geneva, Ignazio Silone in Rome, Leonardo Sciascia in Palermo, Amos Oz in Jerusalem, Haruki Murakami in Tokyo, and many more in the United States, including E. B. White in Maine and Carl Sandburg in North Carolina. These interviews later led to a book that I titled *Word Still Count with Me*, which I published with Norton.

While at the *Times*, I was invited to teach writing at the City College of New York, which I did for two years in the evening session. I admired the men and women in my classes, knowing that most of them came from poor or middle-class families and worked during the day. Later, I was asked to teach a writing seminar at Yale University and did so for a year. I encouraged a few of the talented students to become writers.

All during my professional life as a newspaperman, I have written books. Several of them had connections to my wartime experiences. As an author, I have produced five novels and a dozen books in the fields of American history, biography, reportage, and literature.

My first published book, *Abraham Lincoln: A Press Portrait*, combined my admiration for the sixteenth president and the role newspapers played in his life. (Its original title was *Lincoln As They Saw Him*.) *Abraham Lincoln: A Press Portrait* remains my most enduring work.

One of my headline-making books was—and still is—*Dangerous Dossiers*. It started out as a *New Yorker* article. The book exposes the fact that the FBI kept files on America's greatest authors. As a result, biographers are now aware of the need to use the Freedom of Information Act to obtain government records.

My second novel, *Get These Men Out of the Hot Sun*, an anti-war story, was an effort to expose the duplicity of the Vietnam War. It used real and fictional characters. Two of my novels, *The Montauk Fault* and *Kings in the Counting House*, though thrillers, each used newspapers, television, and international intrigue as characters or background.

In addition to the *New York Times*, my articles and reviews have appeared in *The New Yorker*, *The Nation*, *Newsweek*, *Atlantic Monthly*, *Harper's*, *American Heritage*, *Military History Quarterly*, *Chicago Tribune*, *Washington Post*, *Newsday*, and *Art News*.

In my first effort to write for the theater in 1980, I had a stroke of good fortune. My one-man play, *Mister Lincoln*, had its world premiere in Canada, moved to Ford's Theater in Washington, then went on Broadway, London, Australia, and the Republic of China. It was also presented on national public television. Since its debut, *Mister Lincoln* has never been off the boards; it continues to be performed in colleges and community theaters all over the United States.

With Shirley, and sometimes with our children, we have revisited some of the places where I served during my war. We have toured Sicily and Italy extensively. Once I ascended halfway up Mount Etna—so had a couple of characters in my novel *The Return*.

Because I had written about Italian culture and literature for many years and reviewed and interviewed so many of its distinguished authors, I was decorated as a Knight, Order of Merit, by the Republic of Italy. In the presence of our daughters, Esther and Laura, the Italian cultural counsellor in New York read the citation and gave me the rosette and medallion on behalf of the president of Italy.

I was lucky to be a newsman in khaki on *The Stars and Stripes* during World War II. That experience led me to join the greatest newspaper in the United States. After 47 years of the *New York Times*, I retired in 1995. In recognition of my writings, I was presented with the George Polk career award from the Long Island University.

I still strongly believe that the printed word—in newspapers and books—is essential in all of our lives and the life of the community.

—Herbert Mitgang, New York 2004

A Final Word

AFTER REREADING this personal memoir, I find it necessary to add that I do not wish to leave the impression that war and the military life are fun. I was lucky to spend much of my time in uniform as an Army correspondent, sleeping in a bed rather than in a foxhole, and having the freedom to roam in interesting places. Sometimes I did come under fire—bombed by the Luftwaffe in Algeria and shelled by the Wehrmacht in Tuscany—but going up to the front lines was mainly a matter of choice. My companions on *The Stars and Stripes* were intelligent men and we believed that we contributed to the war effort by putting out a serious newspaper.

While I lived to tell these tales, many GIs had a rough time. On vacation in Italy several years ago, I placed a wreath on the grave of a companion who is interred in an American cemetery above the Anzio beachhead. One of my boyhood friends served in the 82nd Airborne and was wounded twice; long afterward, he lives in a Veterans Administration facility. War leaves wounds, heartbroken parents, widows, and orphans.

As an American and as a student of history, I must add that I believe in the United Nations as the best means to settle disputes, provide justice, and maintain the peace.

Index

★ ★ ★

About the Author

HERBERT MITGANG first served in Air Corps intelligence and then as an Army correspondent and managing editor of the Oran–Casablanca and Sicily editions of *The Stars and Stripes* during World War II. He earned six battle stars.

He is the author of a score of books of fact and fiction, and a Pulitzer Prize finalist in biography. His articles and commentary have appeared in *The New York Times*, *The New Yorker*, *Harper's*, *Atlantic Monthly*, *American Heritage*, *Military History Quarterly*, *The Nation*, *Newsweek*, and *ArtNews* (to which he is a contributing editor).

As an adjunct professor, he has taught writing at Yale University and at City College New York.

A retired book critic and columnist, editorial writer and member of the Editorial Board of *The New York Times*, his writing prizes include the American Bar Association Gavel Award and the George Polk Career Award. For his writings on Italian culture and literature, he was decorated as a knight, Order of Merit, by the Republic of Italy. He is a fellow of the Society of American Historians, Columbia University.